The
Great
Steak
Book

The Great Steak Book

GRADY SPEARS

WITH TORRI RANDALL

PHOTOGRAPHY BY DICK PATRICK

Ten Speed Press

BERKELEY   TORONTO

1⊜
Ten Speed Press
PO Box 7123
Berkeley, California 94707
www.tenspeed.com

Distributed in Australia by Simon and Schuster Australia, in Canada by
Ten Speed Press Canada, in New Zealand by Southern Publishers Group,
in South Africa by Real Books, in Southeast Asia by Berkeley Books, and
in the United Kingdom and Europe by Airlift Book Company.

Cover and Text Design by Catherine Jacobes Design, San Francisco
Food Styling by Trish Dahl
Bottom photographs on pages 1, 19, and 75 © PhotoDisc

Meat supplied for photographs courtesy of the Freedman Meat Company
    and Nolan Ryan's Tender Aged Beef.
Diagram on page 4 courtesy of the California Beef Council.

Library of Congress Cataloging-in-Publication Data
Spears, Grady.
    The great steak book / Grady Spears with Torri Randall.
        p. cm.
    ISBN 1-58008-215-7 (pbk.)
    1. Cookery (Beef) I. Randall, Torri. II. Title.
TX 749.5.B43 S64   2000
641.6'62—dc21   00-032573
First printing, 2000
Printed in Hong Kong

2 3 4 5 6 7 8 9 10—03 02 01

CONTENTS

Publisher's Note

Some of the recipes in this book include raw eggs, meat, or fish. When these foods are consumed raw, there is always the risk that bacteria, which is killed by proper cooking, may be present. For this reason, when serving these foods raw, always buy certified salmonella-free eggs and the freshest meat and fish available from a reliable grocer, storing them in the refrigerator until they are served. Because of the health risks associated with the consumption of bacteria that can be present in raw eggs, meat, and fish, these foods should not be consumed by infants, small children, pregnant women, the elderly, or any people who may be immunocompromised.

Acknowledgments

First, I want to thank Linda Bebee and everyone at the Texas Beef Council and Bruce Berven and everyone at the California Beef Council for all they do to promote beef.

I also want to thank Cody and Teresa Todd for taking me in when I was first struggling in the cattle business; Deb Crockett, for giving me a place to live; the folks at the Vann-Roach Cattle Company (Gary, Weldon, and Roger); Billito and Kathy Donnell; and all the other West Texas ranchers that took me in over the years. These great people taught me everything I know about the cattle business and ranching—this book is for all of you!

I also want to thank Mary Margaret Spikes (you are the best!), my family for supporting me in all the crazy things I do, and my restaurant family for being there and being so committed every single day.

Thanks, too, to Phil Wood and everyone at Ten Speed Press, and especially Dennis (T-Bone) Hayes; thank you for everything you have done to shape not only my career, but also my life.

Both Torri and I would also like to thank all of the cattle men and women all over America, who have persevered year after year, striving against all odds to preserve a vanishing way of life. You are all American heroes.

And most importantly, thank you Sara for never giving up on me!

The Promise of Perfection

"Back when I was punching cows, if you'd told me I was going to be a chef someday, I would have doubled up in laughter and fallen off my horse."

—from A COWBOY IN THE KITCHEN

I was born in Fort Worth, Texas, in 1968, and my family moved about seventy-five miles away, out to Granbury, when I was fourteen years old. I was always hanging out at local ranches, riding horses, and helping with the cattle. The first time I went to a livestock show I just knew I'd be a real cowboy some day. I even joined the local Future Farmers of America and raised a 4H calf that was my pride and joy. When my family moved back to Fort Worth, I was so upset about losing my calf that I talked my folks into letting me stay at my friend's ranch until my freshman year was over. After I did move back to Fort Worth, I got a job working at the stockyards and then a cattle company, working and later brokering cattle.

After some hard times in the cattle business, I got a second job bussing, then waiting tables in a restaurant in Houston. Eventually I got an offer to run a hotel restaurant in Marathon in the beautiful and desolate Trans-Pecos region of West Texas. When the cook quit one day without any notice, and there were about a hundred folks sitting there waiting for their lunch, I had no choice but to head into the kitchen and start cooking. It was do or die time. But it was a great way to learn the business and how to cook, and from there I began to create my own version of cowboy cuisine.

I discovered that what people want is good, honest, wholesome food, without too much fuss. And they want great service in a comfortable environment. In 1995, my partners and I opened our first Reata restaurant in Alpine, near Marathon. Both the restaurant and menu were designed to capture the feeling of an old ranch house, where "customers would feel at home with their spurs on." In 1996, we opened the second Reata, on the thirty-fifth floor of the Bank One Tower in downtown Forth Worth, and in February 2000, we opened Reata Beverly Hills.

Always a cowboy town, the people of Fort Worth seemed to fall in love with our no-nonsense chuckwagon cooking. But I noticed that folks kept asking for one thing in particular, over and over: they wanted a perfect steak. Every time. Not sometimes. Not almost perfect. Perfect Every Time. And so this book is our answer. A great steak is the quintessential American meal. It's what every working cowboy orders on his Saturday night in town. But you don't have to wait 'til Saturday night. You can cook a perfect steak any time, and I promise, it's the easiest thing in the world.

—GRADY SPEARS

A COWBOY'S GUIDE TO GREAT STEAKS

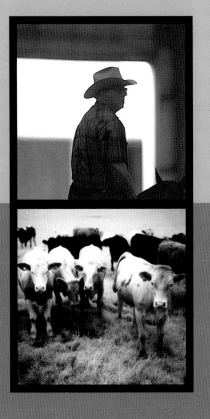

CHAPTER ONE

In American restaurants, people order more than 348 million servings of steak per year, and in American homes, steak is the single most popular beef dish served, accounting for over 18 percent of the beef prepared and eaten at home. I can tell you that an awful lot of steaks are prepared and eaten both in my restaurants and in my own home, because steaks are delicious, easy, and convenient, and the great thing is that there are so many different kinds of steak that there's one to fit any menu and any budget.

After my years in the cattle business and cooking in restaurants, I've learned a few things about steaks—what makes 'em great and how to ruin 'em. (I guess you can take the cowboy off the range, but you can't take the range out of the cowboy, because, yes, a steak is still my favorite thing to eat.)

A Buyer's Guide

When I was a kid, I used to think a steak was just a steak and all meat came wrapped in cellophane. Then after working in the cattle business, I learned that a steer is a very big animal, so there are a whole lot of different parts and pieces, and, in particular, a whole lot of different steak cuts. So many, in fact, that it can be a little bewildering when you head toward the meat counter at the supermarket. Just a generation or two ago every neighborhood had a friendly butcher who knew everything about every cut of meat and exactly how to prepare it and how to cook it. Time was I'd buy something from the store called a steak, take it home and grill it, and end up with something much closer to boot leather than the juicy, tender steak I'd had the weekend before in a restaurant. I knew I hadn't overcooked it, so what was I doing wrong? Well, first of all, I was

Beef Grading

The grading of beef is optional in the United States and is paid for by individual meat packers and meat processors. Beef is graded for quality by the USDA according to standards they have established indicating palatability. There are eight quality grades for beef, but the three usually seen in your supermarket are Prime, Choice, and Select. A number of factors determine quality grades: age, the amount of marbling or intramuscular fat, texture, and color. Young beef with the most marbling is given the highest or prime quality grade and is usually sold to restaurants and specialty meat markets. Choice and Select are the grades most commonly found in supermarkets.

buying the wrong cut. Different cuts, of course, are meant for different cooking methods, and some absolutely need to be marinated first or handled in a certain way for the best results.

I think it's helpful to have a look at a steer to know where the different steaks come from, because there definitely is a pattern. The tenderest steaks come from the parts of the animal that get the least amount of body movement and have less connective tissue (the tenderloin, sirloin, top and short loins, and rib areas). Steaks from areas that experience a lot stress from movement are tougher (chuck, shank, round, and flank).

BEEF STEAKS: WHERE THEY COME FROM

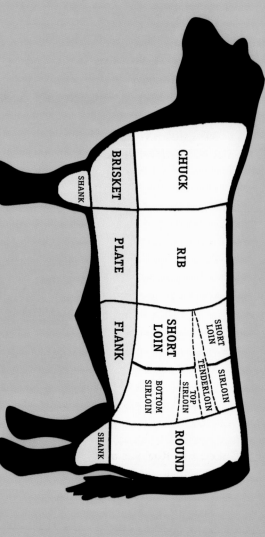

Rib
Rib-Eye Steak, Rib Steak, Spencer Steak, Rolled Rib Roast (boneless), Standing Rib Roast, Prime Rib Roast

Short Loin
Porterhouse Steak, T-Bone Steak, New York Steak, Strip Steak, Kansas City Steak, Beef Cutlets

Sirloin
Top Sirloin Steak, Bottom Sirloin Steak, Tri-tip can be grilled, broiled, or pan-fried. Top sirloin is also ground for burgers and steak tartare.

Plate
Skirt Steak

Tenderloin
Beef Fillet, Filet Mignon, Medallions, Tenderloin Steak, Tenderloin Roast, Chateaubriand

Round
Cubed Steak, Round Roasts, Ground Round

Chuck
Chuck Roast, Short Ribs, Cross Rib Roast

Flank
Flank Steak and London Broil, Flank Roast

Brisket
Brisket

What's What When It Comes to Steaks

Rib-Eye Steak (boneless), Rib Steak (bone-in), and **Spencer Steak (boneless)** vary somewhat in flavor and texture, and the amount of marbling, but are all cut from the choice area of the eye of the rib. They are generally from $1/2$ inch to $1^1/2$ inches thick, or up to 2 inches thick for a bone-in rib steak. All can be grilled, broiled, or pan-fried. These steaks are all tender enough that they don't need marinating, but if you want to use a marinade, do so for no more than 2 hours.

Standing Rib Roast, a rib roast that is still on the bone, is usually served with the bone. Roasts can benefit from glazes and rubs but are too big to be effectively marinated.

Rolled Rib Roast is a rib roast that has been boned, rolled, and tied up with twine, which makes it easier to carve. And, of course, this means more beef per pound, since you're not paying for all those heavy bones.

Prime Rib Roast comes from the rib area farthest from the shoulder. A cut so tender it easily absorbs the flavors of rubs and glazes beautifully, it is also absolutely delicious with just salt and pepper.

T-Bone Steak, from the center of the short loin with the signature T-shaped bone, is big and juicy, and is usually cut $3/4$ inch to 1 inch thick. This is the perfect grilling steak, which is probably why it is so popular at barbecues, but it is also great broiled or pan-fried, and benefits from either marinades and rubs or minimal seasoning.

Porterhouse Steak comes from the large end of the short loin, and also has the T-shaped bone. It can be grilled, broiled, or pan-fried, and benefits from marinades and rubs or just minimal seasoning.

New York, Kansas City, or **Strip Steak** and **Beef Cutlets** come from the small end of the short loin. Restaurant cuts of this steak come with some of the T-shaped bone in, but supermarket cuts are boneless and usually about 1 inch thick. These cuts can be grilled, broiled, or pan-fried, and benefit from either marinades and rubs or minimal seasoning.

Sirloin: Top Sirloin Steak, Bottom Sirloin Steak, and **Tri-tip** are all from the longer area of the loin. Steaks from the sirloin are less tender than those from the short loin, making them perfect candidates for marinades, rubs, and glazes. They can be grilled, broiled, or pan-fried, but I think they lend themselves particularly well to searing on a grill or pan, then finishing in the oven. Top sirloin is also ground for burgers and steak tartare.

The **Tenderloin** is a long, narrow wedge in the center of the sirloin area that widens in the middle and tapers at each end. A tenderloin roast is basically the whole piece, trimmed at one end so that it is uniform in width and produces uniform steaks when carved. It is the most tender part of the beef. **Chateaubriand,** which is usually served in restaurants, comes from the central portion of the tenderloin. **Beef Fillet, Filet Mignon,** and **Medallions** are cut from either side of the Chateaubriand and are really differentiated by size, i.e., beef fillet and filet mignon are the largest in circumference, while medallions are the smallest, cut from each end of the tenderloin. Because they are so tender and flavorful, all of these steaks are generally cut a minimum of 1 inch thick and all the way up to $2^1/2$ inches and need minimal seasoning. If you choose to marinate any of these steaks, do so for no more than 1 hour.

Round: Cubed Steak, Round Roasts, and **Ground Round** are from the back end of the animal and usually used as roasts, chicken-fried steaks, or ground for burgers. (So-called round, Swiss, and rump steaks are steaks in name only; they *must* be braised, as they are not tender enough to cook by dry heat methods such as broiling or grilling.)

Flank: Flank Steak and **London Broil** come from the rear flank area. They are the least tender steaks and *must* be marinated, for at least half a day and preferably overnight, but they can be grilled, broiled, braised, or pan-fried.

Skirt Steak, from the area below the ribs called the plate, can be grilled, broiled, or pan-fried, but like the flank steak, they *must* be marinated for at least half a day and preferably overnight.

Brisket comes from the area under the shoulder of the animal and is used for roasts and for corned beef.

The Most Tender Steak Cuts

Tenderloin Steak

Top Loin Steak

Porterhouse/T-Bone Steak

Rib-Eye Steak

Rib Steak

Top Sirloin Steak

Fat Is Not a Four-Letter Word

Three types of fat are found in beef: the outer, subcutaneous layer that covers the outside of the carcass; the seams of intermuscular fat that are found between the muscle layers; and the fat deposits found within the muscles, known as marbling. Marbling—essential to the quality of any cut of steak—makes a steak more juicy, flavorful, and tender, which is why the better quality cuts tend to have more marbling. Fat-obsessed Americans have forced ranchers and cattle raisers to institute special feeding programs to produce leaner, and unfortunately, less flavorful beef. Unless you're on a prescription diet for a particular medical condition, I encourage you to buy well-marbled beef for those special occasions when flavor really matters.

Aging Beef

Not unlike fine wine, beef benefits enormously from the natural process of aging, especially cuts from the rib and loin areas (rib-eye, porterhouse, T-bone, sirloins, and tenderloin). During aging, the natural enzymes present in the meat act as tenderizers by breaking down certain proteins in the tough muscle fibers.

Commercial beef processors age beef by using two methods, known as dry or wet aging. To dry age, certain cuts of beef are hung in a humidity-controlled room that is refrigerated from 32 to 34 degrees, for fifteen to thirty-six days. Dry aging is typically done by specialty beef purveyors for the restaurant market. Wet aging refers to beef that has been cut up and stored in vacuum-sealed bags and refrigerated at 32 to 34 degrees for anywhere from fourteen to thirty-six days depending on the cut (the tougher the cut, the longer the aging).

What to Look For

Choose steaks that are a bright red with no grayish or brown blotches. Make sure they are firm to the touch, not soft or mushy feeling, and that the package is cold with no holes or tears. Unless you strictly limit your fat intake, always be sure your steaks are well marbled and your roasts have a nice layer of fat around them. A well-marbled steak has thin veins of fat running all through it, and will be tender and flavorful. The blanket of fat around a roast can be trimmed after roasting, but will ensure that your roast is juicy and delicious.

Avoid packages with a lot of juice, or *purge*, which may be an indication of improper storage. Always check the sell-by date so you're not buying a steak that's past its prime. Vacuum packaged beef will be a darker, purplish color, which will turn bright red as soon as it's opened and exposed to air.

And don't feel limited to always buying your steaks at your local supermarket. Specialty markets with first-class meat counters are getting popular again and opening all across the country, and I think it's definitely worth a trip and a little extra money to buy some really great, well-aged steaks. If you don't have a specialty market in your area, then mail order makes a convenient way to buy superior steaks (see page 128 for a list of resources). Either way, I promise that you'll notice the difference.

How Much to Buy

Of course, how big a steak you want to eat is entirely up to you. (The bigger the better if you ask me!) You need to figure that typically, an eight-ounce uncooked steak will yield a six-ounce cooked steak. Four ounces ($1/4$ pound) of boneless, uncooked beef, like hamburger, will yield a three-ounce cooked serving.

Servings per Pound

If you're buying larger amounts or cuts of beef, figure that in the cooking process you will lose two to three ounces per pound. Leaner cuts will shrink less because there is less fat to be lost during cooking.

Handling and Storage

Always store steaks in either the meat compartment or the coldest part of your refrigerator (it should be 35 to 40 degrees) as soon as you bring them home. I always tightly wrap beef up in some extra plastic wrap before I store it so there's no chance of leakage. If you're not going to use the meat within a couple of days of purchasing it, you can freeze it in its original transparent packaging for up to two weeks. Rewrap it in freezer paper or a plastic freezer bag to prevent freezer burn if you're planning to store it for longer. To defrost steaks safely, *always* defrost them in the refrigerator the day before you want to cook them—*never* out at room temperature.

How to Cook the Perfect Steak

Once you've selected your favorite cut, preparing and cooking your steak is easy. Steaks can be grilled, broiled, sautéed, pan-fried, pan-broiled, stir-fried, or braised, depending on the cut, and seasoned with wet rubs, dry rubs, or marinades.

Here are few helpful hints for making a perfect steak every time:

★ Be sure to choose the right cooking method. A good rule of thumb is that tender cuts are perfect for dry heat methods like broiling and grilling. Less tender cuts can also be grilled and broiled if they are marinated first. If you don't have time to marinate, these steaks do well with moist heat methods like braising.

★ Be sure to cook steak at the correct temperature. This is really important and is most often the difference between success and failure.

Too high a temperature can char the outside before the inside is done properly, or it can just overcook the whole thing and you've got boot leather instead of a steak (very disappointing when you've spent a little extra money on a really nice piece of meat and you've been looking forward to dinner all day).

★ These days the cooking times for gas and electric ranges are about the same, but I always keep a separate thermometer in my oven so when I'm preheating it, I don't have to wonder whether or not it's really 500 degrees.

★ The cooking times for Select and Choice grades of beef are about the same, but because Select grades tend to be less juicy, it's easier to overcook them.

★ Trim fat *after* your steaks are cooked to preserve their natural juiciness. Most steaks that you buy in the supermarket have a fat trim of less than $1/4$ inch, and, frankly, I don't think that little fat needs to be trimmed at all.

★ Always use tongs to turn your steak, since a fork will pierce the meat and allow those delicious juices to escape. Turn a chopped steak such as a burger with a spatula for the same reason. And don't do that thing you watched your dad do at family cookouts and barbecues—*don't* flatten your burgers to make them cook quicker. All you're doing is pressing out the juices and creating a dry burger.

★ And finally, particularly if you're grilling or broiling your steaks, prepare your side dishes first. In most cases, your steak is going to be done in just a few minutes and you don't want it to get cold while you're waiting for your baked potato.

Adding Flavor

Sometimes the fanciest seasonings you'll want to put on a steak are salt and pepper. On the other hand, if you want to pump up the flavor, or if you've chosen a cut that would benefit from tenderizing, one of the following methods can do the trick.

MARINADES AND BATHS

A marinade is a seasoned liquid mixture that adds flavor to meat and is sometimes a tenderizer as well. A tenderizing marinade contains a natural food acid like lemon or lime juice, wine or vinegar, or a natural tenderizing enzyme such as those found in papaya, ginger, or pineapple. Most marinade recipes include a little vegetable oil to help the other ingredients stick to the meat and to help the meat brown during cooking. A marinade typically contains enough liquid to penetrate the meat to about $1/4$ inch; allow $1/4$ to $1/2$ cup marinade for 1 to 2 pounds of beef. A bath is a marinade with enough liquid to almost completely submerge the meat.

Whether you are using a marinade or a bath, use a food-safe plastic bag or nonreactive container—and *always* marinate in the refrigerator, never at room temperature. Be sure to turn or stir the meat occasionally to evenly distribute the marinade.

Marinate tender cuts for up to 2 hours, since any longer means the muscle fibers of the meat can begin to break down and get mushy. Really tender cuts like filet mignon don't need any marinating, but if you want to add some extra flavor, marinate for just 15 or 20 minutes—but no longer.

Steaks from less tender cuts should be marinated for between 6 and 12 hours, even up to 24 hours for the least tender cuts (longer than 24 hours and you will end up with mush).

If you want to use your marinade later for basting or as a sauce, reserve a portion of it *before* adding your steaks. If you want to make a sauce from a marinade that has been in contact with uncooked meat, it *must* be brought to a full rolling boil. And remember, *never* save or reuse a marinade.

RUBS, DRY AND WET

A dry rub is a blend of seasonings such as fresh or dried herbs and spices applied to the surface of uncooked meat to add flavor, although they don't do anything to tenderize. There are also wet rubs, which are combinations of seasonings that also contain some vegetable oil, crushed garlic, or mustard. As with marinades, be sure to refrigerate the meat during the curing. A rub can actually be applied to the meat and cooked immediately. Time isn't really a factor because the cooking process causes the flavor absorption.

WOOD CHIPS

Another way to add flavor to beef is to add fragrant wood chips (such as hickory, mesquite, or applewood) or wine or whiskey barrel staves to your fire. These are really great if you're using a gas grill, since gas grills don't add any flavor of their own the way charcoal fires do. You'll need to soak the chips in cold water for a half hour before you use them, drain them, then spread them on a piece of aluminum foil. Remove the cooking grate from the gas grill and turn on the gas jets. Set the foil with the chips over the metal slats or on the lava rocks at one corner of the grill (don't forget your gloves!), and then replace the grate. Wait until the wood begins to smoke before you put your meat on to cook. On a charcoal grill, just sprinkle soaked chips over the charcoal.

Equipment

A word about grills:

There are two types of outdoor grills, the traditional charcoal grill that we all grew up with and the newfangled gas grills. Personally, I love cooking over wood or charcoal because nothing else gives your steak that unique flavor of wood smoke. Of the two, I recommend using charcoal briquettes because they're so much a easier to light and control in terms of heat. (Hardwood burns much hotter and faster, so unless you have the time to practice, stick with charcoal.)

Whichever type of grill you have, you will also need tongs (nice long ones), long heatproof oven mitts (they make extra-long ones specifically for barbecuing), and natural hair basting brushes with wood handles (plastic brushes with synthetic fibers melt).

For a charcoal grill you will need a bag of charcoal, and some lighter fluid will definitely make your life easier. Don't worry, it burns off as the coals heat up—I promise it won't make your steak taste like lighter fluid! To light the grill, first make sure the top and bottom vents are open. If your fire ends up being too hot, you can partially close the bottom damper to regulate the heat, but the top vent should always be open while cooking. Next, spread a single layer of briquettes on the charcoal grate. In the center, place a few pieces of crumpled newspaper, arrange some small dry sticks in a crisscross pattern over the newspaper, then set some more charcoal on top of the sticks. Spray lightly with lighter fluid, and, with either a long fireplace match or an electric starter, light the charcoal, then put the cooking grate in place. Leave the lid off. Never add more lighter fluid once the coals are lit. The coals are ready when they are glowing red with a gray, ashy coating.

You can also use a metal chimney to get your fire going—my dad swears by his. Set the chimney in the middle of the charcoal grate. Put some crumpled newspaper in the bottom of the chimney, fill it up with charcoal, and light the newspaper. In 20 to 30 minutes, the charcoal in the chimney will be perfectly ready. Using your mitts, slowly lift the chimney, allowing the coals to fall across the surface of the grate. Put the cooking grate in place.

In addition to regular charcoal, you can use a number of different hardwood charcoals, such as oak, mesquite, hickory, or applewood, which will impart different flavors to the beef.

If you're using an outdoor gas grill, follow the manufacturer's directions to prep and light your grill. The same goes for indoor electric grills and the gas and electric grills that are a part of many kitchen ranges. You should always read the instructions to be sure you're using any of these grills safely.

Another great tool is the really convenient little cast-iron grill pan that you use on your stove top. When it's too cold outside to fire up the barbecue, you can still enjoy a real grilled steak or hamburger, complete with the hash marks!

Degrees of Doneness

Rare: 140°—Bright red in the middle, turning to pink

Medium rare: 145°—Very pink in the middle, turning to slightly brown

Medium: 160°—Light pink in the middle, turning to brown

Well done: 170°—Steak is uniformly brown

Chopped steaks and beef patties should always be cooked to medium (160°). For steaks that are 1½ inches thick or more, remove them from the heat source when the internal temperature reaches 5 degrees below the desired degree of doneness. Let the steak rest for 5 minutes, then carve. The internal temperature will rise 5 degrees while the steak is resting.

Determining Doneness

There are several ways to tell when your steak is perfectly cooked, just the way you like it. First, how does it look? If you're grilling or broiling, does it have that nice dark crust on the outside? Next, cut a very small slit in the steak to check the color inside near the bone, or near the center or thickest part of a boneless cut. Cube steak and burgers should really always be done to medium (160 degrees) or until the center is a light pink to ensure that any dangerous bacteria such as *E. coli* have been killed.

A digital or dial face instant-read meat thermometer will give you the internal temperature of your steak in just a few seconds, but remember—they aren't heatproof, so you can't leave them in the meat while it's cooking. There are also battery-run electronic thermometers, which actually tell you the degree of doneness rather than give you the internal temperature, and they can even be preset to sound an alarm when the meat has reached the selected temperature.

You can also use the chef's touch method, which takes some practice. Basically you are comparing the way the surface of the steak feels when you touch it with your index finger with the way the skin of your hand feels when it's relaxed, in a loose fist, or tightly clenched. For rare, just let one of your hands hang loose and relaxed. Then touch the area between your thumb and index finger with the index finger of your other hand. It will feel soft and spongy, with very little resistance. A rare steak should feel the same way. For medium rare, make a loose fist with one hand and touch the same spot again with the index finger of your other hand. It should feel springy, offering a bit more resistance, but not hard. For medium, clench one hand in a tight fist and touch the same spot with your finger. It will feel firm, with not much give at all.

You can always check individual recipes for ballpark cooking times, but believe me, after you've done a few steaks and you start to feel comfortable with a particular cooking method, you'll begin to get a sense of when they're done. Before long you'll be an expert.

Probably the most important thing to remember is to never walk away while you're cooking your steak. You can always put it back and cook it a little longer if you take it off too soon, but once it's overdone, well, you just have to get out some steak sauce and tell yourself, "Better luck next time."

STEAKS FROM THE TENDERLOIN

CHAPTER TWO

Pepper-Crusted Tenderloin Steak with Cook's Butter

MAKES 4 SUPERB STEAKS

Reata's signature steak dish demands a nice thick filet mignon, Chateaubriand, or any other steak from the tenderloin. I like mine at least 2 inches thick and about the size of a baseball. I believe the potato was created to go with steak, and any kind will do—mashed, baked, or scalloped.

¹/₃ cup Cracked Pepper (page 95)
4 (10- to 12-ounce) tenderloin steaks
Kosher salt
3 tablespoons vegetable oil
4 slices Cook's Butter, roasted garlic variation
  (page 96)

Preheat the oven to 500°. Gently press the cracked pepper into the steaks to evenly coat. Season the steaks with salt. Heat the oil in a large, heavy sauté pan over high heat until hot, but not smoking, because that means it's starting to burn (the oil is ready when a drop of water sprinkled in it sizzles). Add as many steaks as will fit without overcrowding and sear well, about 3 minutes per side. Transfer the steaks to a baking sheet and sear the remaining steaks. Place the steaks in the oven and cook for about 8 minutes for medium rare.

Serve steaks hot with a slice of garlic butter or your favorite variation.

THE CHATEAUBRIAND, A THICK TENDERLOIN STEAK LARGE ENOUGH FOR TWO PEOPLE, WAS CREATED DURING THE TIME OF NAPOLEON FOR THE GREAT FRENCH STATESMAN FRANÇOIS CHÂTEAUBRIAND.

Medallions of Beef with Spicy Béarnaise Sauce

SERVES 4 (3 MEDALLIONS PER PERSON)

Medallions of beef are small, round thick fillet steaks, usually 3 to 4 ounces each, traditionally cooked in butter and served with a slice of bacon wrapped around them. The key is to cook them hot and fast, so the bacon crisps and the medallions develop a crust on the outside but remain pink and juicy on the inside. I think the addition of a spicy béarnaise sauce gives these steaks a rich, Western flavor.

SPICY BÉARNAISE SAUCE

1/2 cup dry white wine

2 tablespoons white wine vinegar

1 tablespoon finely chopped shallots

1/2 teaspoon Cracked Pepper (page 95)

2 sprigs tarragon, chopped

1 sprig thyme, finely chopped

1 sprig chervil or parsley, finely chopped

Generous dash of cayenne pepper

3 egg yolks

3/4 cup butter, melted

Salt

Freshly ground black pepper

12 slices of bacon

12 (3- to 4-ounce) medallions of beef

1 cup salted butter

To prepare the sauce, combine the wine, vinegar, shallots, cracked pepper, tarragon, thyme, chervil, and cayenne in the top of a double boiler over high heat. Cook until reduced by half, then remove from the heat and set aside to cool. Return the mixture in the double boiler over low heat, and,

continued

whisking constantly, gradually add the egg yolks and melted butter until the mixture is thoroughly incorporated. Season to taste with salt and pepper, plus more cayenne if you like. Keep warm over very low heat until ready to serve.

To prepare the beef, wrap a slice of bacon around each medallion and secure with a toothpick. Depending on the size of your pan, you will probably need to cook them in batches. Cook 4 at a time in $1/4$ cup butter; 6 at a time in $1/2$ cup butter. Heat the correct amount of the butter in a large, heavy sauté pan over high heat until melted and bubbly, but before it turns brown. Add as many medallions as will fit without overcrowding and cook for about 5 minutes per side for medium rare. Serve with the béarnaise sauce spooned over the medallions.

Beef Tenderloin with Tabasco Hollandaise

SERVES 8 TO 10

I love to serve this at small dinner parties because it's so easy to prepare. In addition to over the tenderloin, serve hollandaise on some steamed asparagus or any type of squash, add some roasted potatoes, and you have a feast for you and your friends.

TABASCO HOLLANDAISE

1¹/₄ pounds unsalted butter
4 egg yolks
Juice of 2 limes
2 teaspoons Tabasco sauce
2 teaspoons tomato purée
Kosher salt

¹/₄ cup salt
¹/₂ cup coarsely ground black pepper
1 (4- to 5-pound) beef tenderloin
4 tablespoons vegetable oil

To prepare the hollandaise, slowly melt the butter in a saucepan over low heat, then set aside and let stand for a few minutes to allow the milk solids to settle on the bottom of the pan. Pour the clarified butter from the pan into a separate bowl and set aside. Discard the remaining milk solids. Or you can pour the melted butter through a fine strainer.

Combine the egg yolks, lime juice, Tabasco, tomato purée, and salt in a food processor or blender, and process until well blended. With the machine running, slowly add the clarified butter and process until smooth. Transfer the hollandaise to the top of a double boiler over low

continued

heat to warm. Keep warm (but not hot) until ready to serve.

To prepare the tenderloin, preheat the oven to 500°. In a small bowl, combine the salt and pepper, and then spread the mixture on a baking sheet. Roll the whole tenderloin in the mixture until it is completely coated. Heat the oil in a large skillet or sauté pan over high heat until hot, but not smoking (the oil is ready when a drop of water sprinkled in it sizzles). Wearing oven mitts and using a pair of tongs in each hand, carefully set the whole tenderloin in the hot oil and sear well, 4 to 6 minutes per side. Transfer the tenderloin to a baking sheet. Place the tenderloin in the oven and roast for 20 to 25 minutes, until it reaches an internal temperature of 150° (the bigger end of the tenderloin will be medium rare, the smaller end closer to medium or medium well). Remove the tenderloin from the oven and let stand for 10 minutes, then cut into 8 to 10 slices and, if desired, serve with the warm Tabasco hollandaise.

BEEF IS OFTEN CALLED NUTRIENT-DENSE FOOD, MEANING THAT YOU GET A LOT OF NUTRITIONAL BANG FOR YOUR CALORIE BUCK. A 3-OUNCE SERVING OF BEEF CONTRIBUTES LESS THAN 10 PERCENT OF CALORIES TO A 2,000-CALORIE DIET, YET SUPPLIES MORE THAN 10 PERCENT OF THE DAILY VALUE FOR PROTEIN, ZINC, IRON, NIACIN, VITAMIN B6, AND VITAMIN B12.

Beef Tenderloin
with Tabasco
Hollandaise

Texas Beef Wellington

SERVES 4 TO 6

Beef Wellington is one of those spectacular entrées that will make your guests think you spent all day in the kitchen, but actually it's really very easy to prepare. Folks won't expect the chiles, cheese, and corn inside my take on tradition. I would serve this with a good Mexican beer rather than wine.

2 tablespoons kosher salt

4 tablespoons Cracked Pepper (page 95)

1 (4- to 5-pound) beef tenderloin

4 tablespoons vegetable oil

1 cup fresh corn kernels, puréed

1 1/2 cups grated queso (soft Mexican cheese)

6 poblano chiles, roasted, stemmed, and seeded (page 95), and sliced in half lengthwise

1 (1-pound) package of puff pastry

1/2 cup butter, melted

2 eggs, beaten

Preheat the oven to 400°. In a small bowl, combine the salt and pepper and then spread the mixture on a baking sheet. Roll the whole tenderloin in the mixture until it is completely coated. Heat the oil in a large skillet or sauté pan over high heat until hot, but not smoking (the oil is ready when a drop of water sprinkled in it sizzles). Wearing oven mitts and using a pair of tongs in each hand, carefully set the tenderloin in the hot oil and sear well, 4 to 6 minutes per side. Transfer the tenderloin to a baking sheet. With a spatula, spread the corn purée across the top of the tenderloin from end to end. Sprinkle the grated cheese over the corn, and then arrange the chiles over the cheese so they cover the entire roast.

To wrap the tenderloin in the pastry, butter a large baking sheet. Layer 2 sheets of pastry on the baking sheet. Set the tenderloin on the center of the pastry sheets, then fold the pastry over both sides and the ends of the tenderloin to form a package. Seal the seams with melted butter, and brush the entire package with the beaten eggs. Bake, uncovered, for 20 to 30 minutes, until the pastry is a rich golden brown.

Allow the tenderloin to rest for 10 to 15 minutes before serving. Slice into $1/4$- to $1/2$-inch slices and enjoy the compliments!

Filet Mignon the City Way

SERVES 4

Often called tournedos in French restaurants, the filet mignon is the Rolls-Royce of steaks. I used to call them "tornadoes" when I was a kid, no doubt inspired by the kind that are a regular feature of the weather in West Texas.

4 filets mignons, 1$1/2$ inches thick
Kosher salt
Cracked Pepper (page 95)
4 slices Cook's Butter (page 96), any variation

Preheat the broiler. Rub each filet with salt and pepper, then place them on a broiling pan. Set the pan on the highest rack in the oven (5 to 8 inches below the heat source), and broil 2 to 3 minutes per side to sear. Move the pan to the middle rack and broil 2 minutes longer per side for rare, 3 minutes for medium, and 4 minutes for well done. Serve filets with slices of your favorite Cook's Butter.

Filet Mignon the Cowboy Way

SERVES 4

Nolan Ryan is a Baseball Hall of Fame legend, not to mention a mighty talented cowboy. Nolan recently began his own beef company, Nolan Ryan's Tender Aged Beef, which produces some of the tastiest steaks you'll find anywhere. This recipe for filet mignon from Nolan is a lot like one of his famous fastballs—best served sizzling over the plate!

4 filets mignons, 1^1/$_2$ inches thick
2 tablespoons vegetable oil
Kosher salt
Cracked Pepper (page 95)
4 slices Cook's Butter (page 96), any variation
   (optional)

Prepare the grill according to the directions on page 15. Brush both sides of each filet with oil and then season with salt and cracked pepper. Arrange the filets on the grill rack and grill 5 to 6 minutes on each side for medium rare. Add 2 minutes for medium and another minute or 2 for well done. Serve garnished with slices of your favorite cook's butter.

THE FAMOUS AMERICAN WRITER O'HENRY, IN HIS BOOK *THE FOUR MILLION* (1906), FIRST COINED THE PHRASE *FILET MIGNON* TO DESCRIBE A BONELESS STEAK CUT FROM THE SMALL END OF THE TENDERLOIN. AND ALL THIS TIME I THOUGHT IT WAS INVENTED BY SOME FANCY FRENCH CHEF.

Filet Mignon
the Cowboy Way

Filet Mignon Simmered in Ruby Port

SERVES 4

This rich, elegant variation of filet mignon takes a little longer, but it is really just as easy as grilling or broiling.

4 filets mignons, 2 inches thick
1 teaspoon kosher salt
$1/2$ teaspoon Cracked Pepper (page 95)
$1/4$ cup butter
4 shallots, peeled and halved
1 cup ruby port

Rub the filets with the salt and pepper. Heat the butter in a large, heavy skillet or sauté pan with a tight-fitting lid over high heat until melted and bubbly, but before it turns brown. Add the steaks and sear well, 2 to 3 minutes per side. Add the shallots and the wine, and reduce the heat to low. Cover the skillet and simmer for 30 minutes. Serve the filets with the pan drippings and 2 shallot halves on top of each steak.

Tenderloin Tamales with Sundried Tomato Cream and Pecan Mash

MAKES 26 TAMALES

The next time you're having a party, make these nontraditional tamales and your guests will love you! They are bit labor-intensive, but well worth it, and you can make them a day ahead. And don't be put off because this recipe calls for lard. Vegetable shortening is a fairly recent substitute for lard, which has always been the shortening of choice in ranch kitchens and chuckwagons.

30 corn husks, soaked in hot water until pliable, 1 to 2 hours

MASA FILLING
1 pound masa
3 cups fresh corn kernels (about 6 ears of corn)
1$1/4$ cups lard or vegetable shortening
1 cup chicken stock
$1/2$ cup coarsely chopped fresh cilantro
2 tablespoons salt
2 tablespoons paprika

BEEF FILLING
3 pounds ground tenderloin or sirloin
1 onion, finely chopped
1 red bell pepper, finely chopped
5 jalapeño peppers, stemmed, seeded, and diced
4 cloves garlic, minced
2 tablespoons ground cumin
2 tablespoons salt
1 tablespoon ground coriander

continued

Tenderloin Tamales with Sundried Tomato Cream and Pecan Mash

PECAN MASH
3/4 cup pecan pieces
2 cloves garlic, coarsely chopped
1/2 cup chopped fresh cilantro
3/4 cup freshly grated Parmesan cheese
3 jalapeño peppers, stemmed, seeded, and diced
1 1/2 cups olive oil
Salt

SUNDRIED TOMATO CREAM
1 tablespoon vegetable oil
2 cloves garlic, minced
4 tablespoons butter
1/2 cup rehydrated sundried tomatoes, puréed
  or very finely chopped
1 quart heavy whipping cream
1/2 cup freshly grated Parmesan cheese
Salt
Freshly ground black pepper

To prepare the masa filling, combine all the ingredients in a food processor and process until well blended. The mixture should be the consistency of wet mud. To test, drop a piece into a glass of cold water. If it floats, you have just the right amount of lard. If it sinks, add more lard, 1 tablespoon at a time, mixing well after each addition. Set aside.

To prepare the beef filling, combine all of the ingredients in a large mixing bowl, and mix well. Cover and refrigerate until ready to use.

To prepare the pecan mash, combine the pecans, garlic, cilantro, Parmesan, jalapeños, and 1/4 cup of the olive oil in the bowl of a food processor and pulse to coarsely chop the pecans. With the machine running, slowly add the remaining olive oil through the feed tube and process until it is

continued

completely incorporated. Season to taste with salt. Set aside, or refrigerate until ready to use.

To prepare the sundried tomato cream, heat the oil in a saucepan over medium-high heat until hot. Add the garlic and sauté for about 2 minutes, just until it begins to brown. Add the butter and sundried tomatoes and cook, stirring often, for 1 to 2 minutes longer. Lower the heat to low, add the cream, and simmer, stirring constantly, for 15 to 20 minutes, until the cream has been reduced by half. Add the cheese, season to taste with salt and pepper, and mix well. Remove from the heat and serve warm.

To make the tamales, cut 4 of the softened corn husks into $1/8$-inch-wide strips, then cut each strip in half lengthwise. Set aside. (You should end up with 52 strips. If you don't have quite enough, use string cut to 5-inch lengths).

On a clean, dry work surface, lay out one of the remaining corn husks. Place about 2 tablespoons of the masa filling in the center of the husk, and spread it out to within 2 inches of the edges. Next, place about 3 tablespoons of the beef filling in the center of the masa. Tightly roll the husks up lengthwise around the filling, then twist both ends and tie with the corn husk strips to secure. Repeat with the remaining ingredients.

Place the tamales in a single layer on a steaming rack in a pot with a tight-fitting lid. You may need to cook them in 2 batches. Set the rack of tamales over $1^1/2$ inches of boiling water, cover, and let steam for about 1 hour, adding water as necessary to maintain a $1^1/2$-inch depth. To serve, cut an opening in the top of each tamale with a small sharp knife. Place the tamales on a platter and top with 1 tablespoon each of the pecan mash and tomato cream.

The Bellamy Brothers Santa Fe Chili with Cornbread Croutons

SERVES 4 TO 6

The Bellamy Brothers, Howard and David, are legendary country music performers with numerous hits including the classic, "Let Your Love Flow." Besides writing catchy and clever songs, they also create some tasty dishes. This recipe for a Santa Fe–style chili can be "tuned" up any number of ways by adding other types of chile peppers and beans, and if you prefer, you can substitute other cuts of chopped beef.

CORNBREAD CROUTONS

3 cups cubed day-old cornbread

6 tablespoons vegetable oil

Salt

4 potatoes, cut into 1-inch cubes

4 tablespoons vegetable oil

2 large yellow onions, coarsely chopped

5 cloves garlic, coarsely chopped

2 pounds beef tenderloin, cut into 1-inch cubes

2 cups diced roasted green chiles (page 95)

4 cups beef stock

Kernels from 4 ears corn

Salt

Freshly ground black pepper

1 cup finely chopped fresh cilantro

1 cup grated white cheddar or Monterey jack cheese, for garnish

To prepare the croutons, preheat the oven to 325°. In a large bowl, toss the cornbread cubes with the oil and salt to taste. Place the cubes on an ungreased baking sheet, spaced apart so they are not

continued

touching, and bake for 10 to 15 minutes, until the bread starts to brown and harden. Remove from the oven and let cool for 5 to 10 minutes.

To prepare the chili, in a large pot over high heat, add the potatoes and water to cover and bring to a boil. Cook for 10 to 15 minutes, until the potatoes are just starting to soften. Drain and set aside.

In the same pot, heat the oil over high heat. Add the onions and garlic and sauté for 5 to 8 minutes, until soft and starting to brown. Add the tenderloin pieces and cook for 3 to 5 minutes, until browned on all sides. Add the potatoes and chiles and cook for 2 to 3 minutes longer. Add the beef stock and bring to a boil. Decrease the heat to medium and simmer for 30 to 40 minutes, until the liquid is reduced by half. Stir in the corn kernels and salt and pepper to taste. Cook for 5 minutes longer, remove from the heat, and stir in the cilantro.

Ladle the chili into warmed soup bowls and garnish with the cheese and croutons.

Cowboy Carpaccio

SERVES 4 TO 6 AS AN APPETIZER

This amazing Italian appetizer requires the very best quality cut from the tenderloin—the beef fillet—which you will probably have to special-order. Ask your butcher to trim it for you, and if you're planning to serve it the same day, ask him to slice it as well. Otherwise, sharpen your longest knife to razor-sharpness and go for it. The slices should be so thin that you can almost see through them. As with any beef recipe that is being served uncooked, it is very important that the beef fillet be kept refrigerated from the time you bring it home until you plan to serve it.

1 1/2 pounds trimmed tenderloin, cut into paper-thin slices

3/4 cup Homemade Mayonnaise (page 105)

1 to 2 tablespoons Ranch Worcestershire Sauce (page 106)

1 teaspoon fresh lemon juice

2 to 3 tablespoons milk

Salt

Freshly ground black pepper

On a large serving platter, arrange the carpaccio slices in a single layer with edges overlapping. In a small bowl, whisk together the mayonnaise, Worcestershire, and lemon juice. Whisk in just enough milk to make a thin sauce that will coat the back of a wooden spoon. Season to taste with salt and pepper. Drizzle the sauce in a lattice over the carpaccio. Serve immediately.

Western Steak Tartare

SERVES 4 TO 6 AS AN APPETIZER

The Dijon mustard in this recipe replaces the raw eggs traditionally used as a binding agent in steak tartare and also provides some extra flavor. Try this cowboy version of a classic appetizer at your next cocktail party or breakfast buffet.

2 pounds finely ground, cleaned and trimmed tenderloin

1 red onion, diced

6 tablespoons Dijon mustard

6 jalapeño peppers, stemmed, seeded, and diced

6 tablespoons finely chopped fresh cilantro

Kosher salt

Freshly ground black pepper

Sliced pumpernickel bread, as accompaniment

1 cucumber, unpeeled, thinly sliced, as accompaniment

6 anchovy fillets, as accompaniment (optional)

$3/4$ cup Homemade Horseradish Sauce (page 108), as accompaniment (optional)

In a large mixing bowl, combine the ground beef, onion, mustard, peppers, and cilantro. Using your hands, mix well, making sure everything is evenly distributed. Season with salt and pepper. Shape the steak tartare into a smooth mound in the center of a serving platter. Surround with the pumpernickel, cucumber, and anchovies. Serve the horseradish sauce on the side.

Western Steak
Tartare

Steak and Mushroom Kebabs

SERVES 6

Kebabs are great at a barbecue, served either as an entrée or as an appetizer with your favorite dipping sauce. If you're using bamboo skewers, don't forget to soak them in water for 30 minutes so they don't burn on the grill.

MARINADE

1 cup red wine

1 cup olive oil

2 tablespoons Ranch Worcestershire Sauce (page 106)

2 cloves garlic, chopped

4 tablespoons Homemade Ketchup (page 104)

2 teaspoons sugar

1 teaspoon salt

2 tablespoons balsamic vinegar

1 teaspoon dried marjoram

1 teaspoon dried rosemary

2 pounds tenderloin, cut into 1^1/$_2$-inch cubes

1 pound cremini mushroom caps

2 red onions, cut into 1-inch dice

2 large, ripe but firm tomatoes, cut into 1-inch dice

2 red or green bell peppers, cut into 1-inch dice

To prepare the marinade, whisk together all the ingredients in a large nonreactive bowl until well blended. Add the steak cubes and the mushroom caps to the marinade, mix well, and marinate in the refrigerator for at least 2 hours or up to 4 hours.

continued

Steak and Mushroom Kebabs

To prepare the kebabs, prepare the grill according to the directions on page 15. Alternate the steak cubes, mushrooms, onions, tomatoes, and peppers on the skewers. Grill 2 to 3 minutes per side, and serve either on or off the skewers.

RIB-EYES, T-BONES, SIRLOINS, AND PORTERHOUSE STEAKS

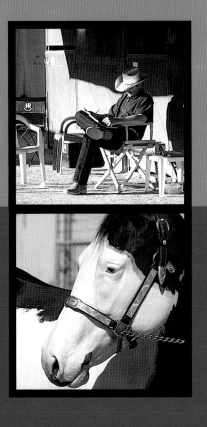

CHAPTER THREE

Pan-Seared Rib-Eye Steaks with Cowboy Coffee Pan Blend

SERVES 4

Your guests won't be able to guess that fresh coffee is the secret ingredient, but they'll love their steaks, and love you for making them! This favorite cowboy rub for steaks is a chuckwagon classic.

COWBOY COFFEE PAN BLEND

1/2 cup freshly ground coffee
1/2 cup coarsely ground black pepper
1/4 cup kosher salt
1/4 cup brown sugar

4 (14- to 16-ounce) rib-eye steaks
2 tablespoons vegetable oil

To prepare the coffee blend, combine all the ingredients in a jar with a tight-fitting lid. Shake well.

To prepare the steaks, preheat the oven to 450°. Season each steak with the coffee blend, evenly coating all sides and edges. Heat the oil in a large, heavy skillet over high heat until just to the smoking point. Add as many steaks to the pan as will fit without overcrowding and sear well, 2 to 3 minutes per side. Transfer the steaks to a baking sheet and repeat with the remaining steaks. Place the steaks in the oven and cook for 5 to 10 minutes for medium rare. Let stand for at least 5 minutes before serving.

Pan-Seared Rib-Eye Steaks with Cowboy Coffee Pan Blend

Rib-Eye Stew

SERVES 4 TO 6

Nothing is more satisfying than hot stew on a cold night served with a basket of fresh biscuits!

5 tablespoons unsalted butter
1 large onion, diced
3 cloves garlic, peeled and minced
2 pounds beef rib-eye, cut into 1-inch cubes
$1/3$ cup flour
2 carrots, peeled and cut into 2-inch dice
1 large potato, peeled and cut into 2-inch dice
1 cup port wine
3 cups beef stock
1 tablespoon dried sage
1 tablespoon dried oregano
Kosher salt
Freshly ground black pepper

In a large stockpot over medium heat, melt the butter. Add the onion and garlic and sauté for 3 to 4 minutes, until soft. Meanwhile, dredge the cubed beef in the flour, coating well on all sides. Add the beef to the stockpot, increase the heat to high, and sauté for 5 minutes, until well browned. (Try to keep the beef cubes from touching each other as much as possible, because if they are overcrowded they will steam rather than brown.) Add the carrots, potato, wine, stock, sage, and oregano and stir well, scraping up any solidified juices from the bottom of the pan. Set the heat to low, cover the pot with a lid just slightly ajar, and simmer for about 40 minutes. Season to taste with salt and pepper and serve in big bowls.

Smoked Prime Rib with Horseradish Sauce

SERVES 8

If you want to serve this for supper, you'll need to start it at noon or so—but it's well worth it. You can use your favorite brands of store-bought sauces if you don't have time to make the home-made recipes, but try them sometime—you'll love the extra flavor they give your cooking.

1 (7- to 8-pound) prime rib roast, trimmed
$3/4$ cup Ranch Worcestershire Sauce (page 106)
$3/4$ cup Homemade Teriyaki Sauce (page 61)
$1^1/_2$ cups Reata Grill Blend (page 94)
$1/_2$ cup sour cream
3 tablespoons Homemade Horseradish Sauce (page 108), plus extra for garnish
Salt

Prepare a fire in a smoker and let it burn down for 20 to 30 minutes. Place either hickory, mesquite, applewood, or your favorite chips on top of the coals. Meanwhile, preheat the oven to 500°. Set the roast in a shallow baking dish. In a bowl, combine the Worcestershire and the teriyaki and pour it over the roast, then cover the roast with the grill blend. Cook the prime rib in the oven for 45 minutes to 1 hour, or until a nice crisp crust forms.

Next, set the roast in the smoker and smoke for 4 to 5 hours, until it reaches an internal temperature of 140° (be sure to check the coals and water every $1^1/_2$ hours or so). Remove the roast from the smoker, transfer it to a platter, and let stand for 30 minutes. Meanwhile, pour the pan juices into a mixing bowl, scraping in any

continued

Smoked Prime Rib with Horseradish Sauce

browned meat bits (which are full of flavor). Add the sour cream and horseradish, mix well, and season to taste with salt. To carve the roast, place it on a board so that the ribs are pointing up. Using a very sharp carving knife, slice the meat away from the bones. Thickness is up to you—I like to cut $1/4$ to $1/2$-inch slices. Serve with the horseradish sauce alongside.

RANCH STEAK BREAKFAST

One of my favorite things to do with leftover prime rib is to slice it very thin and fry it up for breakfast with some eggs and potatoes. First, set the oven to 200°. Then melt 1 tablespoon of butter in a hot skillet and sauté some chopped onion and a little chopped garlic until the onion caramelizes. If you have any leftover roasted or baked potatoes, go ahead and chop them up and toss them in the skillet, adding more butter if necessary. When the potatoes are brown around the edges, transfer them to a serving plate and keep them warm in the oven. Add the sliced steak to the skillet and cook it until heated through (don't overcook it), then transfer it to the serving plate in the oven. Prepare eggs to your liking to serve with the steak and potatoes—and don't forget the fresh hot coffee.

Molasses-Glazed Rib Roast

SERVES 6

Where's the molasses in this glaze recipe? Actually, molasses is a by-product of the refining process of sugar. As the brown sugar melts into the roast, it turns to molasses and makes a great crust on the outside of the roast.

MOLASSES GLAZE
2 cups brown sugar
6 tablespoons kosher salt
4 tablespoons paprika
6 tablespoons coarsely ground black pepper

1 (5- to 6-pound) rib roast
$^1/_2$ cup vegetable oil

Preheat the oven to 500°. To prepare the glaze, combine all the ingredients in a large bowl and mix well.

To prepare the roast, place it in a large roasting pan and rub it all over with the vegetable oil. Using your hands, press the glaze mixture into the roast to completely cover. Cook the roast for 20 to 25 minutes, then lower the temperature to 325° and cook for about 1 hour, until it reaches an internal temperature of 140°. Let stand for 20 to 30 minutes before carving and serving.

Beef Inspection

THE FEDERAL MEAT INSPECTION ACT OF 1906 FIRST MADE INSPECTION MANDATORY FOR ALL MEAT THAT CROSSED STATE LINES. THEN THE WHOLESOME MEAT ACT OF 1967 REQUIRED THAT THE INSPECTION OF MEAT SOLD WITHIN A STATE MEET INSPECTION REQUIREMENTS AT LEAST AS STRINGENT AS THOSE OF THE FEDERAL GOVERNMENT. MEAT INSPECTION ASSURES THAT ALL MEAT IS WHOLESOME AND ACCURATELY LABELED; HOWEVER, IT IS NOT THE SAME AS MEAT GRADING. ALL MEAT SOLD IN THE UNITED STATES MUST BE INSPECTED.

Rib-Eye Steak with Port and Roasted Shallot Sauce

SERVES 4

This easy reduction sauce is perfect over any cut of steak or roast. Serve it over mashed potatoes, alongside some sautéed vegetables and sourdough biscuits warm from the oven.

PORT AND ROASTED SHALLOT SAUCE

6 large shallots (about ¹/₂ pound), peeled and quartered
3 teaspoons olive oil
6 cups (or 1 750-ml bottle) tawny or ruby port
4 tablespoons butter, diced
Salt

4 (10- to 12-ounce) rib-eye steaks
Salt
Freshly ground black pepper

To prepare the sauce, preheat oven to 350°. In a bowl, toss the shallots with the olive oil to evenly coat. Arrange the shallots in a single layer on a baking sheet, cover with foil, and roast for 15 minutes, or until they are soft and just beginning to brown. Let cool, then mash with a fork or purée in a food processor. (They keep for about a week in the fridge.)

In a large saucepan over medium heat, bring the port to a boil and cook until reduced by two-thirds, 30 to 40 minutes. Add 2 tablespoons of the shallots, whisk in the butter, and season to taste with salt. Remove from heat and keep warm.

Season the steaks on both sides with salt and pepper and place in a baking dish. Pour the port sauce over the steaks and refrigerate for 20 to 30 minutes.

continued

Rib-Eye Steak with Port and Roasted Shallot Sauce

To prepare the steaks, preheat the oven to 475°. Heat a grill pan or skillet over high heat until hot. Add the steaks and sear well, 3 to 4 minutes per side. Transfer the steaks to a baking sheet. Place the steaks in the oven and cook for 5 to 6 minutes for medium rare. Let stand for 5 minutes before serving with the warm reserved sauce.

Grilled New York Strip Steak with Chile Butter

SERVES 4

Also known as the Kansas City steak, the shell steak, or the strip steak, depending on where in the country you live, the New York steak is one of the most tender and flavorful. Serve with Dutch Oven Potatoes (page 116) and Creamed Spinach (page 126) for the real "steak house" experience!

4 (10- to 12-ounce) New York strip steaks
Kosher salt
Freshly ground pepper
4 slices Cook's Butter, chile variation
    (page 96)

Prepare the grill according to the directions on page 15. Season the steaks with salt and pepper. Grill the steaks for 6 to 8 minutes per side for medium rare. Serve each steak topped with a slice of the chile butter.

THE NAME "STEAK" COMES FROM THE OLD SAXON WORD "STEIK," WHICH MEANS STICK. WHEN THE SAXONS INVADED GREAT BRITAIN, THEY BROUGHT THEIR CATTLE WITH THEM, ALONG WITH THEIR FAVORITE WAY OF EATING BEEF—ON A POINTED STICK OVER A CAMPFIRE. SOUNDS LIKE THE ORIGINAL BARBECUE, DOESN'T IT? THE WORD "SIRLOIN" COMES FROM THE FRENCH WORD "SURLONGE," WHICH LITERALLY MEANS OVER THE LOIN, WHICH IS, IN FACT, WHERE IT COMES FROM.

Sirloin Picadillo

Sirloin Picadillo

SERVES 4 TO 6

This fast and easy traditional dish from south of the border works for lunch or dinner and is easy to double or triple for a crowd. Serve with flour or corn tortillas, a tossed green salad, and a big pitcher of sangria, and you've got a party!

4 tablespoons vegetable oil

2 red onions, minced

4 cloves garlic, diced

4 jalapeño peppers, stemmed, seeded, and diced

3 pounds sirloin steak, cut into 1-inch cubes

1 cup Chuckwagon Chile Paste (page 110)

1 cup diced ripe tomatoes

1/2 cup chopped fresh cilantro

Salt

Flour or corn tortillas, as accompaniment

Heat the oil in a large, heavy skillet over high heat until hot. Add the onions, garlic, and peppers and sauté for 3 to 4 minutes, until soft. Add the sirloin and sauté for 7 to 8 minutes, until nicely browned. Add the chile sauce and the diced tomatoes, lower the heat, and simmer for 30 to 40 minutes, stirring occasionally, until the meat is tender. Add the cilantro, season to taste with salt, and cook for 5 minutes longer. Serve warm, with warm flour or corn tortillas.

Frontera Steaks with Enchiladas

SERVES 4

Border food is a blend of Texas traditions with the flavors of old Mexico. I can't think of a better border combination than a juicy Texas rib-eye or T-bone with cheesy enchiladas for a stick-to-your-ribs kind of a meal—these are big servings but cowboys are big eaters. The steaks finish cooking in the oven, so time it so you bake the enchiladas at the same time as the steaks go in the oven.

ENCHILADAS

1/2 cup peanut oil

12 corn tortillas

2 cups Chuckwagon Chile Paste (page 110)

1 pound grated Monterey Jack cheese

4 (10- to 12-ounce) rib-eye steaks

4 tablespoons vegetable oil

Salt

Freshly ground black pepper

1 cup Chuckwagon Chile Paste (page 110),
   as accompaniment.

To prepare the enchiladas, preheat the oven to 425°. Heat the oil in a large, heavy skillet over high heat until very hot but not smoking. Oil is ready when a drop of water sprinkled into it sizzles. Using tongs, carefully slide a tortilla into the hot oil and cook for 2 to 3 seconds, just until the tortilla is pliable. Drain on paper towels, and repeat with the remaining tortillas. Cover the bottom of a large casserole dish with 1 cup of the chile paste. Spread the tortillas out on a clean, dry work surface, top each with 2 tablespoons of the grated cheese, and then roll them up.

Arrange the rolled tortillas in a single layer in the casserole, cover them with the remaining chile paste, and sprinkle with the remaining cheese. Bake for about 10 minutes, or until the cheese is melted.

To prepare the steaks, prepare the grill according to the directions on page 15. Preheat the oven to 425°. Rub each steak with 1 tablespoon of the oil and season with salt and pepper to taste. Grill the steaks for 4 to 5 minutes per side. Transfer them to a baking sheet. Place the steaks in the oven and cook for 6 to 8 minutes for medium rare.

Serve each steak topped with 2 of the enchiladas and a generous serving of chile sauce.

Steak Salad

SERVES 2 HUNGRY FOLKS WHO ARE
FEELING A LITTLE CALORIE-CONSCIOUS

This salad makes a satisfying lunch. Some crumbled blue cheese makes a great addition, and you can also modify it by using any of your favorite dressings instead of oil and vinegar. Whatever you choose, just be sure to go easy with it—the steak is pretty juicy, and nothing's worse than a soggy salad.

HOMEMADE CROUTONS

1 cup crusty French or Italian bread, cut into
    1-inch cubes
4 tablespoons olive oil
1 teaspoon garlic powder (optional)
3 teaspoons dried herbs, such as basil, thyme,
    or oregano (optional)

1 (16- to 18-ounce) rib-eye or strip steak
Salt
Freshly ground black pepper
1 teaspoon garlic powder
1 tablespoon butter
1 head crisp romaine lettuce, torn into pieces
1 head butter lettuce, torn into pieces
1 large, ripe tomato, cut into wedges
Olive oil
Balsamic vinegar

To prepare the croutons, preheat the oven to 400°. Toss the bread cubes in a large bowl with the olive oil, garlic powder, and dried herbs to evenly coat the bread. Spread the cubes out on a baking sheet and bake for 15 to 20 minutes, until crunchy and a rich, golden brown. Let cool completely.

continued

Steak Salad

To prepare the steak, season the steak with salt, pepper, and the garlic powder. Heat the butter in a skillet or grill pan over high heat until melted and bubbly, but before it turns brown. Add the rib-eye and sear for about 5 minutes per side for medium rare. Slice the steak across the grain.

To prepare the salad, in a salad bowl, toss together the lettuce, tomato, and oil and vinegar to taste. Add the steak slices, toss well, and season to taste with salt and pepper. Add the croutons just before serving and you're good to go.

Branded Beef

BRANDED BEEF IS AVAILABLE IN MANY UPSCALE SUPERMARKETS, SPECIALTY MEAT MARKETS, AND BY MAIL ORDER. CERTIFIED HEREFORD, CERTIFIED ANGUS, AND NOLAN RYAN'S TENDER AGED BEEF ARE SOME OF THE MORE FAMILIAR BRAND NAMES CURRENTLY AVAILABLE. BRANDED BEEF COMPANIES CARRY THE GRADING PROCESS BEYOND THE USDA GRADING SYSTEM. AFTER THE USDA GRADES THE BEEF, THE BRAND NAME GRADERS MAKE THEIR SELECTIONS, CHOOSING MEAT THAT FITS THEIR INDIVIDUAL PROGRAMS OF MARBLING AND QUALITY. BRANDED BEEF IS A LITTLE MORE EXPENSIVE, BUT IT IS THE VERY BEST YOU CAN BUY.

Grilled Teriyaki Steaks

SERVES 4

Teriyaki sauce is so versatile it tastes great on beef, poultry, or fish. It should be fairly thick to use as a glaze, but I like to thin it slightly with a little pineapple juice for a lighter sauce. Go ahead and make a double batch so you will have some on hand when you need to pull a dinner together quickly. (It keeps for up to 7 days in an airtight container in the refrigerator.)

HOMEMADE TERIYAKI SAUCE

1 cup soy sauce
$1/2$ cup brown sugar
2 tablespoons minced garlic
2 tablespoons peeled, minced fresh ginger

4 (12- to 14-ounce) sirloin steaks
Salt
Freshly ground black pepper

To prepare the teriyaki sauce, vigorously whisk together all the sauce ingredients in a bowl.

To prepare the steaks, place them in a baking dish. Pour 1 cup of the teriyaki over the steaks (reserving the remaining $1/4$ cup), and turn the steaks to evenly coat. Refrigerate for at least 2 hours, but no longer than 4 hours. Prepare the grill according to the directions on page 15, and preheat the oven to 475°. Season the steaks with salt and pepper and grill for 3 to 4 minutes per side. Transfer the steaks to a baking sheet and brush them with the remaining teriyaki sauce. Place the steaks in the oven and cook for 5 to 6 minutes for medium rare. Let stand for 5 minutes before serving.

Grilled T-Bone Steaks with Honey-Mustard Glaze

SERVES 4

The T-bone is the favorite cowboy steak. When I was working cattle for a living, I always looked forward to my Saturday night steak dinner. I didn't have a lot of money in those days, so I always ordered a T-bone because it really gives you a lot of bang for your buck.

HONEY-MUSTARD GLAZE
Juice of 2 limes
$1/8$ cup olive oil
1 tablespoon Ranch Worcestershire Sauce
   (page 106)
1 tablespoon minced garlic
$1/3$ cup Dijon mustard
$1/3$ cup honey

4 (16-ounce) T-bone steaks
Salt
Freshly ground black pepper

To prepare the glaze, whisk together all the ingredients in a mixing bowl until well blended. Set aside.

To prepare the steaks, prepare the grill according to the directions on page 15 and preheat the oven to 475°. Meanwhile, season the steaks well with salt and pepper and place them in a baking dish. Pour $3/4$ cup of the glaze over the steaks (reserving the remaining $1/4$ cup), and turn the steaks to evenly coat. Set aside for 15 to 20 minutes. Grill the steaks for 3 to 4 minutes per side. Transfer the steaks to a baking sheet, and brush them with the remaining glaze. Place the steaks in the oven and cook for 5 to 6 minutes for medium rare. Let stand for 5 minutes before serving.

Grilled T-Bone Steaks with Honey-Mustard Glaze

Pan-Seared Porterhouse Steaks

SERVES 4

The porterhouse is a big, hearty steak that will satisfy your hungriest guest. Some brown mushrooms sautéed in butter and your favorite style of potatoes make great companions to this ranch house favorite.

4 (16-ounce) porterhouse steaks
Salt
Freshly ground black pepper
3 tablespoons vegetable oil
1 cup diced red onion
1 large, ripe tomato, diced
4 jalapeño peppers, stemmed, seeded, and diced
2 cloves garlic, minced
1/4 cup apple cider vinegar
1/4 cup chopped fresh cilantro

Preheat the oven to 475°. Season each steak on both sides with salt and pepper. Heat the oil in a large, heavy skillet over high heat, until just to the smoking point. (If you don't have a large enough skillet to do all the steaks at once, you can do them in batches or one at a time, dividing the remaining ingredients accordingly.) Using a pair of tongs, carefully place the steaks in the pan and sear for 3 minutes on one side. Turn the steaks over, add the onion, tomato, peppers, and garlic, and sauté for 3 to 4 minutes. Add the vinegar and cilantro and continue to cook for 3 minutes longer. Transfer the steaks to a large baking pan, and pour the vegetable mixture over the steaks. Place the steaks in the oven and cook for 7 to 8 minutes for medium rare. Serve with the vegetables and pan drippings poured over the steaks, open a bottle of red wine, and enjoy.

Border Beef Tips

SERVES 6

This is another great border union. I like to serve this with a big platter of Spanish-style rice, refried beans, and some warm flour tortillas.

3 tablespoons vegetable oil

3 pounds rib-eye, cut into 2-inch cubes

$1/2$ cup butter

1 red onion, chopped

4 cloves garlic, minced

4 ripe tomatoes, diced

6 jalapeño peppers, stemmed, seeded, and diced

1 bunch cilantro, chopped

Salt

Freshly ground black pepper

Heat the oil in a large, heavy skillet over high heat until hot. Add the beef and sauté for 4 to 5 minutes, until browned. Remove the beef from the pan and set aside. Add the butter to the hot skillet and heat until melted. Add the onion and garlic, sauté until softened, then add the tomatoes and the peppers, lower the heat to medium, and cook, stirring occasionally, for 5 to 6 minutes, until the vegetables are soft. Return the beef to the skillet and cook, stirring occasionally, 8 to 10 minutes longer. Remove from the heat, fold in the cilantro, and season to taste with salt and pepper.

THE SALISBURY STEAK WAS NAMED AFTER A NINETEENTH-CENTURY ENGLISH DOCTOR, DR. J. H. SALISBURY, WHO ADVISED HIS PATIENTS THAT CHOPPED OR MINCED BEEF SHOULD BE EATEN EVERY DAY TO PREVENT ALL KINDS OF DISEASES.

The Cowboy New York Strip Steak Sandwich

MAKES 4 SANDWICHES

East meets West in this deliciously sophisti-cated sandwich, which I like to serve with a salad of fresh field greens and some fried pota-toes. Some Tomato Jam (page 100) spread on the sandwich rolls works really well with this recipe, as do the Jalapeño Jam (page 99) and Onion Marmalade (page 101).

MARINADE
3/4 cup olive oil

2 cloves garlic, minced

1 teaspoon sugar

4 (8- to 10-ounce) New York strip steaks

1 tablespoon olive oil

4 tablespoons butter

1 red onion, sliced

2 jalapeño peppers, stemmed, seeded, and
   cut into thin strips

4 Kaiser or sourdough rolls

Salt

Freshly ground black pepper

To prepare the marinade, whisk together all the ingredients in a bowl until well blended. Place the steaks in a single layer in a shallow baking dish, pour the marinade over the top, and turn the steaks to evenly coat. Marinate the steaks in the refrigerator for at least 4 hours but no more than 24 hours. Remove 1/2 hour before cooking to allow to return to room temperature.

To prepare the sandwiches, heat the olive oil and 2 tablespoons of the butter in a large, heavy skil-let over high heat until hot. Add the onion, lower

continued

The Cowboy New York Strip Steak Sandwich

the heat to medium, and sauté for about 15 minutes, or until the onion begins to caramelize. Add the peppers, cook for 1 minute, then remove the vegetables from the pan and set aside. Heat the remaining 2 tablespoons of butter in the hot skillet over high heat until melted and bubbly, but before it turns brown. Add the steaks and pan-fry for 5 to 6 minutes per side for medium rare.

To serve, slice the steaks very thin across the grain. Divide the steak among the sandwich rolls, top each with the onions and peppers, and season with salt and pepper.

IN 1814, MARTIN MORRISON BEGAN TO SERVE HIS CUSTOMERS STEAK AND ALE WHEN THEY STOPPED OVERNIGHT AT HIS NEW YORK CITY INN, OR PORTER HOUSE. HIS STEAKS BECAME SO POPULAR THAT SOON OTHER INNKEEPERS WERE INCLUDING STEAKS ON THEIR MENUS, AND THE PARTICULAR CUT BECAME KNOWN AS THE PORTERHOUSE.

Cowgirl Steak Diane

SERVES 4

This is my variation on the traditional Steak Diane. If you use a less expensive cut than strip sirloin, first marinate it overnight in a red-wine-based marinade (1 cup red wine, 1/2 cup brown sugar, 1/2 cup soy sauce, and salt and pepper to taste). The key to this dish is to cook the steaks quickly in a very hot skillet so they retain their tenderness.

4 (12- to 14-ounce) well-marbled strip sirloin
     steaks, cut 1/2 inch thick
2 tablespoons butter
2 tablespoons vegetable oil
2 tablespoons brandy
2 tablespoons minced shallots or scallions
1 (10-ounce) can beef consommé, chilled
1 tablespoon chopped fresh parsley
Salt
Freshly ground black pepper

Preheat the oven to 200°. Place an ovenproof platter in the oven to warm. Using a mallet, pound the steaks to 1/4 inch thick. Pierce one side of the steaks with the tines of a fork, and then roll them up.

Heat the butter and oil in a large, heavy skillet over high heat, until just to the smoking point. Using a pair of tongs, unroll 1 steak into the hot skillet. Cook for 1 minute per side, then transfer the steak to the warm platter. Repeat with the remaining steaks. Return all four steaks to the skillet over high heat. Pour the brandy over the steaks. Using a long kitchen match, ignite the brandy, then gently shake the skillet to extinguish the flame. Lower the heat and cook for 1 minute.

continued

Add the shallots, stir, and cook for 2 minutes. Slowly add the consommé, one spoonful at a time, and increase the heat to bring the mixture to a boil. Spoon 2 tablespoons of the pan liquid onto the warm platter. Transfer the steaks to the platter and keep warm. Cook the pan liquid over medium-high heat until it is reduced by half, about 5 minutes. Add the parsley and season to taste with salt and pepper. Pour the sauce over the steaks and serve immediately.

STEAK DIANE WAS FIRST CREATED AT THE FAMOUS COPACABANA IN RIO DE JANEIRO, BUT NO ONE SEEMS TO REMEMBER WHO DIANE WAS.

Chicken-Fried Steak with Sage Cream Gravy

SERVES 4 TO 6

The fried steak originated in the Deep South and migrated West with the pioneers. Serving potatoes of some sort are a must if you're going for tradition, and if you have time, whip up some buttermilk biscuits, too. Not for folks on a diet, chicken-fried steak is a once-in-a-while treat—it's like a trip back in time to an era when calories didn't count and no one could spell "cholesterol." The Sage Cream Gravy brings an unusual desert flavor to this traditional ranch favorite.

SAGE CREAM GRAVY

1/3 cup unsalted butter

6 tablespoons all-purpose flour

2 1/2 cups whole milk

2 teaspoons kosher salt

2 teaspoons julienned fresh sage

2 teaspoons Tabasco sauce

1 1/4 cups all-purpose flour

3 tablespoons kosher salt

3 tablespoons freshly ground black pepper

2 eggs

1/2 cup buttermilk

Peanut oil, for deep-frying

6 (6- to 8-ounce) beef cutlets

To prepare the gravy, melt the butter in a saucepan over low heat. Slowly add the flour, whisking constantly until a roux forms, 3 to 5 minutes. Add the milk while continuing to whisk. Add the salt, sage, and Tabasco and, whisking constantly, simmer until thickened, 3 to 5 minutes longer. Keep warm in the top of a double boiler set over low heat.

continued

Chicken-Fried
    Steak with Sage
Cream Gravy

To prepare the cutlets, combine the flour, salt, and pepper in a shallow dish or bowl. In a separate bowl, whisk together the eggs and the buttermilk. Heat 1 inch of oil in a large, heavy skillet over high heat until it reaches 375°, or until the oil sizzles when a drop of water is sprinkled into it. Meanwhile, dredge the beef in the flour, coating it completely. Then dredge in the egg mixture and then again through the flour. Repeat this process until the cutlets are all thoroughly coated. Using a pair of tongs, carefully place as many cutlets as will fit in the skillet without overcrowding and fry for 3 to 4 minutes per side, until the crust is crisp and brown. Drain on paper towels, and repeat with the remaining cutlets. Serve piping hot with the sage cream gravy on the side.

Country-Fried Steak with Red-Eye Gravy

SERVES 4

A customer from Kentucky ordered a chicken-fried steak and told me, "That was the best fried chicken I ever ate!" Evidently in Kentucky they call it "country-fried steak" so nobody confuses it with fried chicken!

1 cup all-purpose flour
1 teaspoon kosher salt
1 teaspoon coarsely ground black pepper
3 eggs
Peanut oil, for deep-frying
4 (6- to 8-ounce) beef cutlets
1 cup whole milk
1¼ cups strong black coffee

In a shallow dish or bowl, combine ¾ cup of the flour, the kosher salt, and the coarsely ground pepper. In a separate bowl, beat the eggs. Heat 1 inch of oil in a large Dutch oven or skillet over high heat until it reaches 375°. Meanwhile, dredge the cutlets through the flour mixture, then through the eggs, then back through the flour. Using a pair of tongs, carefully place as many cutlets as will fit in the Dutch oven without overcrowding and fry for 3 to 4 minutes per side, or until the crust is crisp and brown. Drain on paper towels, then repeat with the remaining cutlets.

Lower the heat, add the reserved ¼ cup flour to the remaining oil in the skillet, and stir to form a roux, 3 to 5 minutes. Slowly add the milk and the coffee and, whisking constantly, simmer until thickened, 3 to 5 minutes longer.

Serve the cutlets with the gravy poured over the top.

FLANK STEAKS, SKIRT STEAKS, BURGERS, AND SANDWICHES

CHAPTER FOUR

Flank Steak in Orange, Garlic, and Chile Marinade

SERVES 4 TO 6

The secret to a really tender, delicious flank steak is simple: always marinate, and for all day, if possible.

ORANGE, GARLIC, AND CHILE MARINADE

2 cups freshly squeezed orange juice

Juice of 3 limes

2 teaspoons crushed red pepper flakes

2 teaspoons crushed garlic

$1/2$ cup hoisin sauce

1 tablespoon chopped cilantro

1 (2- to 3-pound) flank or skirt steak

To prepare the marinade, whisk together all of the ingredients in a large bowl until well blended. Place the steak in a large, shallow, non-reactive pan, pour the marinade over the top, and turn the steaks to evenly coat. Marinate the steak in the refrigerator for at least 6 hours.

To prepare the steak, preheat the broiler. Place the flank steak on a broiling pan (reserving the marinade). Set the pan on the highest rack in the oven (5 to 8 inches below the heat source), and broil about 5 minutes per side for rare (if you cook it too much it will become quite tough). While the steak is cooking, pour the reserved marinade into a saucepan over high heat, bring to a rolling boil, and boil for 5 minutes.

To serve, slice the steak very thin across the grain. Serve with the marinade on the side.

Texas London Broil

SERVES 8

This recipe is a variation on the original. I like jalapeños on just about everything, so feel free to back off a little on the peppers if you don't want such a spicy steak.

MARINADE

1 cup vegetable oil

1 cup dry red wine

4 tablespoons soy sauce

2 tablespoons chopped scallions, green and
  white parts

4 jalapeño peppers, stemmed, seeded, and diced

1 clove garlic, minced

1 teaspoon salt

1/4 teaspoon freshly ground black pepper

2 (2-pound) flank steaks

To prepare the marinade, whisk together all of the ingredients in a bowl until well blended. Place the steaks in a single layer in a large, shallow, nonreactive pan, pour the marinade over the top, and turn the steaks to evenly coat. Marinate the steaks in the refrigerator for at least 6 hours, and preferably overnight.

To prepare the steaks, preheat the broiler. Place the steaks on a broiling pan. Set the pan on the highest rack in the oven (5 to 8 inches below the heat source), and, basting with marinade once on each side, broil for 5 to 7 minutes per side.

To serve, slice the steak very thin across the grain.

Rolled Flank Steak Roast with Mushroom Stuffing

SERVES 4 TO 6

The roast is a staple of chuckwagon cooking, and the flank steak makes the perfect rolled roast. All kinds of different stuffing mixtures will work, so don't be afraid to experiment. This one is rich and savory, and really pretty quick and easy when you don't have a lot of prep time.

MUSHROOM STUFFING

2 tablespoons vegetable oil

1 onion, diced

$1/4$ pound cremini or porcini mushrooms, diced

$1/4$ cup minced fresh parsley

2 tablespoons minced fresh chives

1 tablespoon tomato paste

$1/4$ cup dried bread crumbs

$1/4$ teaspoon salt

$1/4$ teaspoon freshly ground black pepper

1 teaspoon paprika

1 (2-pound) flank steak, cut 1 inch thick

1 teaspoon salt, plus extra for seasoning

1 teaspoon white pepper

2 teaspoons Dijon mustard

3 strips bacon, diced

1 onion minced

1 cup hot beef broth

2 tablespoons ketchup

Freshly ground black pepper

To prepare the stuffing, heat the oil in a large, heavy skillet over medium-high heat. Add the onion and sauté until lightly browned. Add the mushrooms and sauté for 5 minutes until the mushrooms start to lose their firmness.

continued

Rolled Flank Steak Roast with Mushroom Stuffing

Remove skillet from the heat, stir in the parsley, chives, tomato paste, and bread crumbs, then season with the salt, pepper, and paprika.

To prepare the flank steak roast, season the steak on both sides with salt and pepper. Spread one side with 1 teaspoon of the mustard. Spread the stuffing evenly over the mustard, and carefully roll up the steak jelly-roll style. Tie securely with string. Set aside.

In a Dutch oven or heavy casserole over medium-high heat, cook the bacon until it is about halfway done, then add the onion and sauté about 8 minutes until caramelized, or well-browned and soft. Place the roast in the Dutch oven and brown on all sides, about 10 minutes total. Add the beef broth, cover the Dutch oven with the lid, and simmer over low heat for 1 hour. Transfer the roast to a warm serving platter. Whisk the remaining 1 teaspoon mustard and ketchup into the pan juices, and season to taste with salt and pepper. Cut the string off of the roast and slice very thin across the grain of the meat. Serve with the sauce poured over the top.

Cuba Libre Flank Steak

SERVES 4 TO 6

In Mexico, when you order a "cuba libre" in a bar you get a rum and Coke. In this recipe, the acid in the Coke tenderizes the meat and the sugar caramelizes on the grill, creating a sweet crust on the outside of the steak. The longer you marinate the meat the better, but discard the marinade afterwards because the Coke goes flat. I like to serve this with rice and warm flour tortillas for the perfect fajitas.

CUBA LIBRE MARINADE

1 cup spiced rum

3 cups cola

Juice of 4 limes

2 (1¹/₂-pound) flank or skirt steaks

4 tablespoons Reata Grill Blend (page 94)

To prepare the marinade, whisk together all of the ingredients in a bowl until well blended. Place the steaks in a single layer in a large, shallow, nonreactive pan, pour the marinade over the top, and turn the steaks to evenly coat. Marinate the steaks in the refrigerator for 4 to 6 hours, or preferably overnight.

To prepare the steaks, prepare the grill according to the directions on page 15, or if you are using a grill pan on the stove top, heat it over high heat until hot. Remove the steak from the marinade (discard the marinade), season on both sides with the grill blend, and grill for 4 to 6 minutes per side for medium rare. Let stand for about 5 minutes before slicing very thin across the grain.

Beef Brisket with Lone Star Wet Rub

SERVES 6 TO 8

Brisket is a less expensive cut that will stretch your steak budget without compromising flavor. Slow cooking is the secret to a tender, juicy roast. This one will take half the day to cook, so get started at noon to have it ready in time for supper. Lone Star is my favorite beer, but any dark beer will work. Hot Slaw (page 123) and baked or mashed potatoes make fine accompaniments.

1 (6- to 7-pound) beef brisket
2 (12-ounce) bottles Lone Star beer, or any
    dark beer
1$^1/_2$ cups Chuckwagon Chile Paste (page 110)
1$^1/_4$ cups brown sugar
Kosher salt

Preheat the oven to 325°. Place the brisket in a large baking dish. In a large mixing bowl, combine the beer, chile paste, sugar, and salt. Using a brush, generously paint the brisket with the wet rub, reserving half. Tightly cover the brisket in foil. Roast the brisket in the oven for 6 to 8 hours, until tender. Every hour, open the foil and baste the brisket with the reserved wet rub until it is all used (being sure the meat is cooked for some time after the last basting). Remove the roast from the oven and let stand, uncovered, for 30 minutes before serving. Slice the brisket very thin across the grain and serve with the pan drippings on the side.

Beef Brisket with
Lone Star Wet Rub

Dutch Oven Skirt Steak with Whiskey Glaze

SERVES 4

The original Dutch oven—a three-footed, cast-iron pot with a unique concave lid—was first brought to the West by traveling Dutch peddlers. The one-pot meal originated in the Dutch oven, because it can be used to cook just about anything over an open fire. You can fry eggs and bacon, bake bread, biscuits, or even a cake, simmer a soup or stew, or cook a roast in this indispensable pot. In addition to the outdoor variety, there is also the flat-bottomed kind that sits on the stove top or goes in the oven.

WHISKEY GLAZE
1 tablespoon vegetable oil
$1/_4$ pound bacon, diced
1 small onion, diced
1 tomato, chopped
1 jalapeño, stemmed, seeded, and diced
1 clove garlic, minced
$1/_4$ cup ketchup
1 tablespoon bourbon
1 tablespoon red chile paste
1 tablespoon brown sugar
1 tablespoon Dijon mustard
1 tablespoon Worcestershire sauce

2 pounds skirt steak
Salt
Freshly ground black pepper
2 tablespoons vegetable oil

To prepare the glaze, heat the oil in a large saucepan over high heat until hot. Add the bacon and sauté until almost done, then add the onion, tomato, jalapeño, and garlic and sauté until the vegetables are soft, 3 to 4 minutes. Add the remaining ingredients, lower the heat to simmer, and cook 10 minutes longer. Remove from heat and set aside. Glaze should be thick and shiny.

To prepare the steaks, place them in a large baking dish or casserole, pour the glaze over the top, and turn the steaks to evenly coat. Marinate the steaks in the refrigerator for at least 2 hours, but no longer than 4 hours. Remove the steaks from the marinade (reserve the marinade) and season on both sides with salt and pepper. Heat the oil in a Dutch oven over high heat until just to the smoking point. Using a pair of tongs, carefully add the steaks and sear for 2 minutes per side. Lower the heat to medium, pour the reserved marinade over the steaks, and cook for 15 to 20 minutes longer for medium rare. Serve hot.

Ranch Meatloaf

Ranch Meatloaf

SERVES 4

Meatloaf used to be a catch-all for leftovers of all kinds of meats. I've seen old recipes that call for beef, pork, and veal all in the same loaf, but for me, there's no substitute for beef!

1 pound ground sirloin
1 egg
$1/4$ cup milk
$1/2$ cup dry bread crumbs
$1/2$ cup chopped onion
2 jalapeño peppers, stemmed, seeded, and diced
$1/2$ teaspoon salt
1 teaspoon Ranch Worcestershire Sauce
** (page 106)**
$1/4$ teaspoon pepper
1 cup tomato sauce
1 cup grated sharp Cheddar cheese
1 cup evaporated milk

Preheat the oven to 350°. In a bowl, combine the sirloin, egg, milk, bread crumbs, onion, jalapeños, salt, Worcestershire, and pepper and mix well. Shape the mixture into a ring, place it in the center of a 2-quart casserole dish, and pour the tomato sauce over the top. Bake the meatloaf for 45 minutes to 1 hour. The meatloaf is done when it is firm to the touch, and the internal temperature reads 160° on a meat thermometer. Remove from the oven and set aside. Preheat the broiler.

In a small saucepan over medium heat, whisk together the cheese and the evaporated milk until well blended. Pour the cheese mixture over the meatloaf. Broil for 5 minutes, or until the cheese is bubbly. Serve hot.

Sirloin Steak Sandwich

MAKES 4 TO 6 SANDWICHES

I know it seems like a lot of trouble to cook a steak just to make a sandwich, but when you're really hungry, a hot sandwich hits the spot like nothing else. And it really isn't that much work. This recipe should take about 15 minutes from start to finish.

4 tablespoons butter

2 red onions, thinly sliced

3 cloves garlic, minced

1 jalapeño pepper, stemmed, seeded, and diced

1^1/$_2$ pounds sirloin steak, thinly sliced

1 cup sliced mushrooms

Tabasco sauce or your favorite hot sauce

4 to 6 Kaiser rolls

In a large, heavy skillet over medium-high heat, melt the butter. Add the onions, garlic, and jalapeño and sauté for 7 to 8 minutes, until the onions are soft. Add the steak and mushrooms and cook 5 to 6 minutes longer, until the meat is cooked through and the mushrooms are soft. Season to taste with Tabasco. Serve immediately on warm rolls.

PHILLY CHEESE STEAK SANDWICH

To make this traditional favorite, follow the recipe for the Sirloin Steak Sandwich. Substitute 1 green bell pepper for the jalapeño, and the hot sauce is optional. Assemble the sandwiches, place them open-faced on a baking sheet, and sprinkle 2 tablespoons of grated Cheddar cheese over both halves of each sandwich. Set them under a preheated broiler for 1 or 2 minutes, until the cheese melts. Close the sandwiches and serve warm.

Philly Cheese
Steak Sandwich

Molasses Rub Sirloin Steak Sandwich

MAKES 4 TO 6 SANDWICHES

Perfect for barbecue picnics, this is one of my favorite all-time sandwiches. The brown sugar in the rub will caramelize and create a fantastic sweet crust on the outside of the meat. Marinate the steak the night before and you'll be good to go. Serve with your favorite condiments such as sautéed onions or some Onion Marmalade (page 101).

MOLASSES RUB

1 cup packed brown sugar
2 tablespoons molasses
2 teaspoons paprika
2 teaspoons dried thyme leaves
1^1/$_2$ teaspoons kosher salt
1^1/$_2$ teaspoons freshly ground black pepper
1 teaspoon garlic powder

2 pounds sirloin steak
4 to 6 tablespoons unsalted butter
4 to 6 sweet or sourdough sandwich rolls

To prepare the rub, combine all the ingredients in the bowl of a food processor and process until the mixture is well blended. The rub can be prepared in advance and stored in an airtight container until ready to use.

Using your hands, completely cover the steaks with the rub, place them on a plate, cover with plastic wrap, and refrigerate for 2 to 4 hours. Remove the steaks from the refrigerator and allow them to return to room temperature while you prepare the grill according to the directions on page 15. Grill the sirloin for 6 to 8 minutes per side for medium rare.

To serve, slice the steaks very thin across the grain. Spread 1 tablespoon butter on each roll and toast them on the grill for a minute or so, then assemble sandwiches.

LIKE EVERYTHING ELSE, QUALITY MAKES ALL THE DIFFERENCE. FOR SANDWICHES AND BURGERS, REALLY CRISP ICEBERG OR ROMAINE LETTUCE AND VINE-RIPENED TOMATOES ARE BEST. IF YOU DON'T GROW YOUR OWN TOMATOES, HERE'S A TIP FOR "MAKING" GREAT TOMATOES. PICK OUT THE VERY BEST LOOKING TOMATOES YOU CAN FIND—THE DEEPEST RED WITH NO BRUISES OR BLEMISHES—EVEN IF THEY ARE HARD AS ROCKS. WHEN YOU GET THEM HOME, LEAVE THEM OUT ON YOUR KITCHEN COUNTER OR ON A WINDOW SILL TO RIPEN—AND I PROMISE, THEY WILL RIPEN. DON'T PILE THEM UP IN A BOWL, THOUGH, SPREAD THEM OUT SO THEY DON'T TOUCH EACH OTHER. PILING FRUIT AND VEGETABLES IN BOWLS IS GREAT FOR WHEN YOU WANT TO PAINT A STILL-LIFE, BUT IT'S NO GOOD FOR GETTING YOUR OUT-OF-SEASON FRUIT OR VEGETABLES RIPE!

The Ranch Burger

SERVES 4

Burgers, like most things in life, are only as good as what they are made of. If you use the best-quality ground sirloin, and you don't overcook them, your burgers will always be delicious. We serve these ever-popular burgers in our restaurants and have perfected them over time. Trust me—these are the best! For cheeseburgers, place slices of Cheddar, Swiss, or Monterey jack on the burgers about 5 minutes before removing them from the oven or grill.

2 pounds lean ground sirloin

2 eggs, beaten

4 tablespoons Reata Grill Blend (page 94)

1 tablespoon oil

4 hamburger buns

Preheat the oven to 400°. Using your hands, thoroughly combine the beef, eggs, and grill blend in a large bowl. Form the mixture into 4 patties and set aside. Heat the oil in a large, heavy skillet over high heat until just to the smoking point. Add the patties and sear for 4 to 5 minutes per side. Transfer the patties to a baking sheet and bake for 6 to 8 minutes for medium rare or 8 to 10 minutes for medium. Serve hot on buns.

VARIATION: THE PERFECT GRILLED BURGER

Prepare your charcoal or gas grill. Follow the recipe for the Ranch Burger. When the grill is ready, place the burgers on the grill and cook with the lid off. Now just leave them be (don't touch or press them) to cook for 6 minutes on each side for medium rare. Serve on buns with all your favorite fixin's.

BASICS, FIXIN'S, AND SIDES

CHAPTER FIVE

Reata Grill Blend

MAKES 1 CUP

I know it seems like unnecessary work to make a spice mix when you can buy all kinds of them already made, but this one is so easy and less expensive than the store-bought kind—and it has no MSG! Keep some in a jar in your pantry, and you'll find yourself using it on everything from burgers and meatloaf to your Sunday roast.

4 tablespoons kosher salt
3 tablespoons pasilla chile powder
2 tablespoons dried granulated garlic
2 tablespoons sugar
2 tablespoons ground cumin
2 tablespoons coarsely ground black pepper
1 tablespoon ground thyme

In a small bowl, combine all the ingredients, blending well to evenly distribute the spices and break up any chunks. Store at room temperature in an airtight container, and don't forget to shake or stir before each use. Keeps for up to three months.

Roasted Chile and Red Bell Peppers

Roasting chiles and red bell peppers adds a nice flavor to many dishes. The key is to watch the peppers closely as broiling is quick. You want the peppers charred, but not burnt to a crisp.

Preheat broiler. Place peppers in a roasting pan and roast in broiler until charred all over. Transfer to a bowl and cover tightly with plastic wrap. Let steam for 15 minutes. Peel peppers (skin will lift away easily). Stem and remove seeds, and slice or leave whole, as the recipe calls for.

Cracked Pepper

The aroma and flavor of cracked pepper is very different from freshly ground pepper, and it's really worth keeping some around for cooking special cuts of beef.

To make cracked pepper, you need to crush each peppercorn into several pieces. One way to do this is to spread peppercorns out in the bottom of a large frying pan, and then crush them with another smaller pan. Sounds easy enough, but it takes a lot more strength than you might think.

The easiest method is to put the peppercorns in a food processor and pulse it once or twice. You'll have to pick through the cracked peppercorns and remove the whole ones, and then repeat the process. It takes a little time and patience, but I promise it's worth it. And the good news is that they will last indefinitely in an airtight glass jar.

Standard Steak Bath

MAKES 3 CUPS

The difference between a marinade and a bath is the amount of liquid. A marinade is only meant to penetrate into the meat about ¹/₄ inch. A bath is made with enough liquid to actually submerge the meat, but you should only leave meat in it for a maximum of 45 minutes.

1 cup Ranch Worcestershire Sauce (page 106)
  or bottled Worcestershire sauce
2 cups vegetable oil

In a large bowl, whisk together the Worcestershire and the oil until well blended. Store in an airtight container at room temperature until ready to use. Keeps for up to 2 months in an airtight container in the refrigerator.

Cook's Butters

Flavored butter is one of my favorite steak toppings. It's easy to make and adds a unique touch of color and flavor to a simple grilled or fried steak. Just blend the seasonings with softened butter, and then freeze it into a cylinder that's ready to slice whenever you need it. These are some of my favorites, but go ahead and experiment to find your own favorite flavors.

ROASTED GARLIC BUTTER
You will need to make the garlic purée first—I like to make enough to fill up a jar to keep around whenever I need it. It will keep for a couple of weeks in an airtight container in the refrigerator, just don't forget to pull it out an hour before you want to use it to let it return to room temperature.

Roasted Garlic Purée

3 whole heads garlic
3 tablespoons olive oil
1 sprig thyme, stems removed

Preheat the oven to 350°. Peel away any excess outer skin from the garlic heads and cut off the top $1/2$ to 1 inch of each to expose the top of the cloves. Set the heads in a small baking dish or on a piece of foil. Drizzle the heads with the oil and sprinkle with thyme. Wrap the heads tightly in aluminum foil and bake for 45 minutes to 1 hour, until the garlic is soft and aromatic. Let cool slightly. Gently squeeze the cloves out of their peels and mash them with a fork or purée in a food processor.

1 cup unsalted butter, softened
2 tablespoons garlic purée
Kosher salt

In a mixer fitted with the paddle attachment, combine the butter, and garlic purée, and process at medium speed until the butter is light and fluffy. Season to taste with kosher salt, and process to mix. Remove the butter from the bowl, place on a length of foil or parchment, and roll up into a $1^1/2$-inch-wide cylinder, squeezing gently as you roll to remove any air pockets. Store in the freezer for up to three months. Just before serving, let butter thaw for 10 minutes, then slice.

VARIATIONS

For all of the variations, follow the directions for Roasted Garlic Butter.

THYME BUTTER

1 cup unsalted butter, softened

1 cup fresh thyme leaves, very finely chopped
   by hand or in a food processor

Kosher salt

CHILE BUTTER

1 cup unsalted butter, softened

5 teaspoons freshly ground pasilla, ancho,
   or guajillo powder

Kosher salt

Freshly ground black pepper

CILANTRO BUTTER

1 cup unsalted butter, softened

2 cups loosely packed cilantro leaves

Kosher salt

LIME BUTTER

1 cup unsalted butter, softened

Juice of 3 limes

Kosher salt

Jalapeño Jam

MAKES 6 CUPS

We use this as a glaze for grilled steaks at the restaurant, but it's fantastic on fresh hot biscuits, too!

12 jalapeños, stemmed, seeded, and chopped
1¹/₂ cups cider vinegar
6 cups sugar
6 ounces liquid pectin

Place the jalapeños in a blender or food processor. Add the vinegar and purée. Transfer the mixture to a large saucepan over medium heat, and whisk in the sugar. Bring to a boil and continue to cook 5 minutes longer, or until the sugar has completely dissolved. Remove from the heat and set aside to cool for 10 minutes, then whisk in the liquid pectin. Using a large spoon, skim any foam from the surface of the jelly, then pour the jelly into sterilized 8-ounce jars. Seal and store in the refrigerator until ready to use.

Tomato Jam

MAKES 2 CUPS

Got more tomatoes in your garden then you know what to do with? Make up some of this jam and spread it on crostini as an appetizer to serve those unexpected guests.

2 tablespoons vegetable oil
1 red onion, diced
2 cloves garlic, minced
2 pounds ripe tomatoes, cored and diced
3 tablespoons brown sugar
Salt
Freshly ground black pepper

Heat the oil in a saucepan over high heat until hot. Add the onion and garlic and sauté for 4 to 5 minutes, or until soft. Add the tomatoes, lower the heat to medium, and cook for 10 to 15 minutes, stirring occasionally. Add the brown sugar and simmer over low heat for 15 to 20 minutes longer, or until thick. Season to taste with salt and pepper. Store in a jar in the refrigerator for up to two weeks.

Onion Marmalade

MAKES 5 CUPS

This is one of my all-time favorite relishes. It's perfect for steak sandwiches, burgers, and any kind of hot dog or sausage.

3 tablespoons olive oil

2 large red onions (about 1$^{1}/_{2}$ pounds), julienned

2 large yellow onions (about 1$^{1}/_{2}$ pounds), julienned

4 bunches scallions, green part only, thinly sliced

1$^{1}/_{2}$ cups balsamic vinegar

$^{1}/_{4}$ cup brown sugar

Kosher salt

Freshly ground black pepper

Heat the olive oil in a large skillet over medium heat until hot. Add the onions and scallions and sauté for about 5 minutes until they begin to soften. Cover the skillet and cook until onions are wilted, about 8 minutes longer. Remove the lid, increase the heat to high, add the vinegar, and cook, stirring occasionally, until the liquid is reduced by half, about 8 minutes. Add the sugar, season to taste with salt and pepper, stir, and taste: it should be sweet and sour. Adjust the sugar to the desired degree of sweetness. Lower the heat and continue cooking until liquid is almost absorbed and the marmalade is thick, about 10 minutes. Remove from the heat and serve warm. Store in a jar in the refrigerator for up to a week.

Homemade Steak Sauce

MAKES 1 CUP

Some people think it's a sacrilege to put steak sauce or ketchup on a good cut of beef, but not when they're homemade! A great sauce enhances a great steak and can transform a burger or a sandwich into a gourmet experience.

2 tablespoons butter
2 onions, finely chopped
$1/_2$ cup dry white wine
1 tablespoon finely minced fresh parsley
Salt
Freshly ground black pepper

In a saucepan over medium heat, melt the butter. Add the onions and sauté until golden brown. Add the wine, lower the heat, and simmer until the liquid is reduced by half, about 5 minutes. Add the parsley and season to taste with salt and pepper. Keeps for up to a week in the refrigerator in an airtight container, and can be used right from the fridge or warmed slightly in the microwave.

Almost Homemade Steak Sauce

MAKES 1 1/2 CUPS

This is really great on burgers and sandwiches, and I love it on fries.

1 cup mayonnaise
1/4 cup cider vinegar
1/4 cup bottled barbecue sauce
2 tablespoons Worcestershire sauce
2 tablespoons honey
Salt
Freshly ground black pepper

In a bowl, thoroughly combine the mayonnaise, vinegar, barbecue sauce, Worcesteshire, and honey, and season to taste with salt and pepper. Store in an airtight container in the refrigerator for up to a week.

Homemade Ketchup

MAKES 3 CUPS

Why make your own ketchup? Because it's so much richer than anything you can buy at the store, and you can control the thickness.

4 tablespoons vegetable oil
10 ripe tomatoes, chopped
2 red onions, diced
5 cloves garlic, crushed
1 cup cider vinegar
1 cup brown sugar
Salt

Heat the oil in a large saucepan over medium-high heat until hot. Add the tomatoes, onions, and garlic and sauté for 3 to 4 minutes. Lower the heat to a simmer and cook 30 to 40 minutes, stirring occasionally. Pour the mixture through a food mill or a strainer and discard the pulp. Return the mixture to the saucepan, place it over medium heat, and cook until reduced by half, 10 to 15 minutes. Add the vinegar and brown sugar and cook 20 to 30 minutes longer, or until it reaches your desired consistency—thick or thin, you choose! Season to taste with salt. Keeps indefinitely in an airtight bottle or jar in the refrigerator.

Homemade Mayonnaise

MAKES 2 CUPS

Not for the calorie-conscious, but for special occasions, homemade mayo is worth it.

3 egg yolks
Juice of 1 lemon
1³/₄ cups vegetable oil
Salt
Ground black pepper

In a blender combine the egg yolks and lemon juice and process until mixed. With the motor running on low speed, slowly pour the oil through the feed tube in a thin stream and process until smooth. Season to taste with salt and pepper, and thin with 1 tablespoon of water at a time if necessary. Keeps for a week in an airtight container in the refrigerator.

VARIATIONS

You can add 1 tablespoon of canned chipotle chiles in adobo sauce to the egg yolk–lemon juice mixture to create a lively mayo for burgers and sandwiches. Or add 1 tablespoon roasted garlic to make an aioli sauce to serve with grilled asparagus or broccoli, or any grilled vegetable. Try experimenting with some of your favorite herbs, such as cilantro, to give your sandwiches a Western flair.

Ranch Worcestershire Sauce

MAKES 1 1/2 CUPS

Worcestershire sauce is a British concoction that was inspired by exotic flavors and spices gathered from all over the Empire. My favorite store-bought brand is Lea & Perrins, but I also like to make my own. This version needs to cure for a couple of weeks, so be sure to make it before you need it.

1 onion, finely chopped

2 cloves garlic, crushed

3 tablespoons yellow or brown mustard seeds

1/2 teaspoon crushed red pepper flakes

1 1/4-inch slice peeled, fresh ginger

1 teaspoon whole peppercorns

1 cinnamon stick

1 teaspoon whole cloves

1/2 teaspoon cardamom seeds

2 cups cider vinegar

1/2 cup molasses

1/2 cup soy sauce

1/2 cup tamarind pulp

1/2 cup water

3 tablespoons salt

1 whole anchovy, mashed

1/2 teaspoon curry powder

On a 12-inch-square piece of cheesecloth, place the onion, garlic, mustard seeds, red pepper flakes, ginger, peppercorns, cinnamon stick, cloves, and cardamom seeds and tie the cheesecloth into a small, tight bag with a piece of string. Place the spice bag in a large saucepan over high heat with the vinegar, molasses, soy sauce, and tamarind. Bring to a boil, then lower the heat and simmer for 45 minutes until thickened. In a bowl, combine the water, salt, anchovy, and curry powder, add it to the reduced liquid in the saucepan, mix well, and remove from the heat. Pour the mixture, including the spice bag, into a nonreactive glass or stainless steel container. Cover tightly and refrigerate for 2 weeks, stirring the mixture and squeezing the spice bag occasionally. After 2 weeks, remove and discard the spice bag and place the sauce in a jar or bottle. Shake well before using.

USING WHATEVER IS AT HAND IS THE ESSENCE OF COWBOY COOKING. CATTLE DRIVES OFTEN TOOK MONTHS, SO CHUCKWAGON COOKS, WITH LIMITED ACCESS TO FRESH SUPPLIES, HAD TO GET CREATIVE WITH WHATEVER THEY COULD FIND. RANCH COOKS HAD A SIMILAR CHALLENGE, BECAUSE TRIPS TO TOWN FOR SUPPLIES DIDN'T HAPPEN VERY OFTEN WHEN TOWN WAS MANY MILES AWAY.

Homemade Horseradish Sauce

MAKES 2 CUPS

Horseradish was made to go with roast beef. This sauce looks as elegant as the traditional kind, but has even more of a bite to wake up anything from a steak sandwich to prime rib.

1¹/₂ cups sour cream
¹/₂ cup mayonnaise
6 tablespoons prepared horseradish
2 teaspoons crushed red pepper flakes
Kosher salt

In a bowl, thoroughly combine the sour cream, mayonnaise, horseradish, and pepper flakes, and season to taste with salt. Store in an airtight container in the refrigerator.

Fruit Mustard

MAKES 1 1/2 CUPS

I use this on all kinds of sandwiches, and I sometimes I whisk in a little oil and cider vinegar to create a refreshing salad dressing.

1 cup Dijon mustard
1/4 cup apricot preserves
1/4 cup honey
3 tablespoons finely diced scallion
3 jalapeño peppers, stemmed, seeded, and finely diced
1/2 sweet red bell pepper, seeded and finely diced
3 tablespoons fresh chopped cilantro
Salt

In a bowl, thoroughly combine the mustard, preserves, honey, scallion, jalapeños, bell pepper, and cilantro, and season to taste with salt. Store in an airtight container in the refrigerator until ready to use.

Chuckwagon Chile Paste

MAKES 5 CUPS

Many regular supermarkets carry all kinds of specialty ingredients these days, so in most parts of the country you don't have to find a Mexican market to buy an array of chiles. I still love to go to the local Mexican store and markets for inspiration whenever I have the time. Don't be afraid to try different chiles to create different tastes and textures. For a hotter, smokier flavor, add 1 or more canned chipotle chiles in adobo sauce just before you begin to purée.

4 ancho chiles, stemmed and seeded
4 New Mexican dried chiles or Mexican guajillos
3 cups chicken stock
$1/2$ white onion, diced
3 cloves garlic, minced

In a large saucepan over high heat, combine the chiles, chicken stock, onion, and garlic. Bring to a boil, then lower the heat and simmer for about 15 minutes, or until the dried chiles have softened. Carefully transfer the mixture to a food processor or blender and purée. Keeps indefinitely in an airtight container in the refrigerator.

Bread and Butter Pickles

MAKES 2 QUARTS

The most popular pickle in ranch houses in west Texas, we serve these with all our sandwiches and burgers at the Reata restaurants.

2 pounds small pickling cucumbers, cut on the diagonal into $1/8$-inch-thick slices (about 5 cups)

1 sweet onion, such as Vidalia or Maui, cut into $1/8$-inch-thick slices

5 cloves garlic, thinly sliced

4 cups cider vinegar

4 cups packed brown sugar

$1^1/2$ tablespoons black peppercorns

1 tablespoon dried dill

$1^1/2$ tablespoons yellow mustard seeds

1 tablespoon whole allspice

1 teaspoon ground cardamom

$1/2$ teaspoon whole cloves

4 serrano chiles or other small hot red peppers

2 bay leaves

$1/2$ teaspoon ground turmeric

1 tablespoon kosher salt

Place the cucumbers, onion, and garlic in a large nonreactive glass or stainless steel bowl and set aside. In a large saucepan over high heat, combine all the remaining ingredients, and bring just to a boil. Carefully pour the hot liquid over the cucumber mixture, and let cool to room temperature. Transfer the pickles to sterilized glass storage jars with tight-fitting lids and refrigerate for 24 hours before serving. These pickles will keep indefinitely in the refrigerator, but they're so good, they won't last long at all!

Pickles and Relishes

BECAUSE OF THE COMPLETE LACK OF OR VERY LIMITED REFRIGERATION AVAILABLE TO OLD-TIME CHUCKWAGON AND RANCH COOKS, PICKLING BECAME ONE OF THE BEST AND TASTIEST WAYS TO PRESERVE THE FLAVORS AND TEXTURES OF VEGETABLES AND SERVE THEM ANY TIME. THERE ARE ALMOST AS MANY VARIETIES OF PICKLES AS THERE ARE VEGETABLES. IN FACT, MY RULE OF THUMB IS, IF YOU CAN GROW IT, YOU CAN PROB-ABLY PICKLE IT! SO BE BRAVE AND TRY PICKLING SOMETHING OTHER THAN CUCUMBERS.

Mashers

SERVES 4

This recipe multiplies beautifully and reheats in the microwave perfectly. You can make a double or triple batch (or more) the day before a party, and then all you have to do is grill your steaks!

2 pounds russet potatoes, peeled and cut into large dice
15 cloves garlic, crushed
5 tablespoons unsalted butter
³/₄ cup heavy whipping cream
Kosher salt
Freshly ground black pepper

Place the potatoes and garlic in a stockpot. Add enough cold water to cover the potatoes by 1 inch, and bring to a boil over high heat. Lower the heat to medium, cover the pot with a lid, and cook 15 to 20 minutes, until the potatoes are just tender. Meanwhile, in a small saucepan over low heat, combine the butter and cream and simmer until reduced by one-quarter.

Drain the potatoes and mash them with the gar-lic. Add the hot cream mixture, and continue mashing until thoroughly combined. Season to taste with salt and pepper and serve at once, or keep warm, in the top of a double boiler until ready to serve.

MASHER VARIATIONS

For **Blue Cheese Mashers,** follow the recipe for Mashers, but omit the garlic and fold 1 cup of crumbled blue cheese into the hot potatoes before serving.

For **Green Mashers,** follow the recipe for Mashers, but omit the garlic. Combine 3 coarsely chopped scallions with 1 tablespoon of melted butter in a food processor or blender; purée to a paste and then combine with the cream before adding to the potatoes.

Onion Fans

SERVES 4

These are so easy and go great alongside any kind of steak sandwich or burger.

4 medium red onions
Sprigs of rosemary or thyme
Olive oil
Balsamic vinegar
Salt
Freshly ground black pepper

Preheat the oven to 350°. Using a thin, sharp knife, make several slices almost all the way through each onion, stopping about $1/8$ inch from the edge. Wedge the sprigs of herbs in the cuts, drizzle the onions with the oil and vinegar, and season with salt and pepper. Wrap each onion in aluminum foil and roast for 45 minutes to 1 hour, until the onions are soft. Serve warm.

Cast-Iron Potatoes

SERVES 4

These are the perfect breakfast potatoes. I like to make them on Sunday mornings with a couple of poached eggs and pan-fried steak.

2 pounds white, yellow, or red potatoes, cut into large dice
5 cloves garlic
2 tablespoons butter
1 red onion, diced

Place the potatoes and garlic in a large stockpot. Add enough cold water to cover the potatoes by 1 inch, and bring to a boil over high heat. Lower the heat to medium, and cook for 15 to 20 minutes, or until the potatoes are just tender. Drain the potatoes in a colander and strain out the garlic cloves. Mash the garlic and coarsely chop the potatoes. Melt the butter over medium heat in a large cast-iron skillet. Add the onion and sauté 2 to 3 minutes, until soft. Add the potatoes and garlic, increase the heat to medium-high, and sauté until crispy and golden. Serve hot.

Twice-Baked Potatoes with Two Cheeses

SERVES 8

These can be a meal in themselves, but they go with any roast or steak. Be sure to use russet potatoes, which have thicker skins than the creamier yellow or white potatoes.

8 large russet potatoes, scrubbed but not peeled

4 tablespoons butter, melted

Salt

$1/2$ cup butter

2 cloves garlic, minced

2 cups heavy whipping cream

Freshly ground black pepper

$1 1/2$ cups grated Monterey jack cheese

$3/4$ cup goat cheese, crumbled

Preheat the oven to 375°. Puncture each potato several times with a fork. Brush with the melted butter and season with salt. Place the potatoes on a baking sheet and bake for 1 hour, or until tender. Remove from the oven and let cool slightly. Slice each potato in half lengthwise and scoop out the middle, reserving the flesh and setting aside the skins.

Melt the remaining $1/2$ cup butter in a saucepan over medium heat, add the garlic, and sauté until soft and brown. Lower the heat, add the cream, and simmer until reduced by one-half. Increase the oven temperature to 425°. In a large bowl, gently fold the reduced cream mixture into the potato flesh and combine thoroughly (do not overmix). Season to taste with salt and pepper. Fill each potato skin with the filling and place on a baking sheet. Sprinkle the cheeses equally over the tops of the potatoes and bake for about 10 minutes, or until the cheese begins to brown. Serve hot.

Dutch Oven Potatoes

SERVES 4

This cowboy classic is the perfect thing to serve with any roast, and even poultry or pork. Paper-thin slices of potato make all the difference; a mandoline is the perfect tool for this, but if you don't have one, use a heavy, sharp knife. If you don't have a Dutch oven, use an 8-inch-square baking dish.

4 tablespoons unsalted butter, diced

2 pounds russet potatoes, scrubbed and cut crosswise into 1/16-inch-thick slices

1 1/2 cups grated Parmesan cheese

Kosher salt

Freshly ground black pepper

2 1/2 cups heavy whipping cream

1 tablespoon minced scallions, for garnish

Preheat the oven to 300°. Butter the bottom and sides of a Dutch oven or baking dish with 1 tablespoon of the butter. Layer one-fifth of the sliced potatoes into the baking dish, making 2 overlapping layers. Sprinkle with 1/4 cup of the Parmesan cheese. Season with salt and pepper and top with 1/2 cup of the cream. Repeat this 4 more times. Top with the remaining butter. Sprinkle with the remaining cheese and cover with foil. Bake for 2 hours, then uncover and bake 15 minutes longer, until the top is lightly browned. For a browner top crust, set the pan under the preheated broiler for just a few minutes. Remove the potatoes from the oven and let sit for 15 minutes before serving garnished with the scallions.

Dutch Oven
       Potatoes

Crispy Papas Fritas

SERVES 4

The best tool for creating potato matchsticks is a handy thing called a mandoline. I have no idea why it's called that, because I don't think it looks anything like the musical instrument, but you can get one at specialty gourmet shops and mail-order catalogs. It's important to let the cut potatoes sit in a bath of cold water to draw out the starch, so they will fry up nice and crisp and won't become a soggy mess.

**4 large russet potatoes, peeled and cut into
 $1/4$-inch-thick matchsticks**
Peanut oil, for deep-frying
1 cup Reata Grill Blend (page 94)

Place the potatoes in a large bowl, add enough cold water to cover, and soak for $1/2$ hour. Heat 1 inch of oil in a Dutch oven or deep, heavy skillet until it reaches 400°. While the oil is heating, drain the potatoes well in a colander and pat dry with paper towels. Divide the potatoes into 3 batches. Add each batch one at a time to the hot oil and cook for 2 to 3 minutes, until they turn a light golden color. Using a slotted spoon, remove the potatoes from the oil and drain on paper towels, reserving the oil in the skillet. Transfer the potatoes to a covered container and place in the freezer for at least 30 minutes or up to an hour, until they are cold but not frozen.

Reheat the oil to 350°. Add the chilled potatoes to the hot oil and refry for 2 to 3 minutes, until they turn a rich golden brown. Drain the potatoes on paper towels, and season to taste with the grill blend. Serve piping hot.

Dutch Oven Cornbread

SERVES 6 TO 8

Cornbread baked in a Dutch oven is still made by chuckwagon cooks on ranches all over Texas and the Southwest.

1 cup flour

1 cup fine yellow cornmeal

1 tablespoon salt

1 tablespoon baking powder

4 jalapeño peppers, stemmed, seeded, and diced

$1/4$ cup finely chopped red onion

$1/4$ cup roasted shallots (page 51), (optional)

3 eggs

$1^1/4$ cups buttermilk

$1/2$ cup butter

Preheat the oven to 375°. In a large mixing bowl, thoroughly combine the flour, cornmeal, salt, baking powder, peppers, onion, and shallots. In a separate bowl, beat the eggs, then whisk in the buttermilk until combined. Fold the egg batter into the dry mixture and combine. In a Dutch oven over medium-high heat, melt the butter. Pour the cornbread batter into the hot butter and increase the heat to high. Cook, without stirring, for 3 to 4 minutes to brown the bottom. Place the Dutch oven in the oven and bake, uncovered, for 30 to 40 minutes, until a toothpick inserted into the center comes out clean. After the cornbread is done, turn it out of the Dutch oven and let cool for a few minutes before slicing.

Blue Cheese Biscuit Pudding

SERVES 6 TO 8

This is the perfect thing to make with leftover biscuits, assuming you have any. Serve with brisket and you'll die happy.

2 tablespoons butter

$1/2$ cup fresh corn kernels

$1/4$ cup diced red bell pepper

$1/4$ cup diced, seeded jalapeño pepper

3 eggs

3 cups crumbled buttermilk biscuits

$1^1/2$ cups heavy whipping cream

$3/4$ cup crumbled blue cheese

Salt

Preheat the oven to 375°. Grease a 2-quart baking dish or casserole. In a large, heavy skillet over medium-high heat, melt the butter. Add the corn kernels, bell pepper, and jalapeño pepper and sauté until soft. Remove from the heat and let cool. In a large bowl, beat the eggs, then add the crumbled biscuits, cream, blue cheese, and the cooled corn mixture. Mix well and season with salt. Pour the mixture into the prepared baking dish and bake for 25 to 35 minutes, until the pudding has set. Scoop out servings with a spoon and serve hot.

Blue Cheese
         Biscuit Pudding

Buttermilk Biscuits

MAKES 20 BISCUITS

Biscuits are served for breakfast, lunch, and dinner in West Texas, and always fresh and hot from the oven. Nothing makes a better sandwich than a buttermilk biscuit and nothing goes better with steak and potatoes. Don't be afraid to use lard— it's what makes biscuits light.

3 1/2 cups flour

3/4 cup lard or vegetable shortening

4 teaspoons baking powder

1 teaspoon baking soda

2 tablespoons sugar

1/2 cups buttermilk

Preheat the oven to 400°. Line a baking sheet with parchment paper or butter it, and set aside. In a large bowl, using a fork or pastry cutter, thoroughly combine the flour, lard, baking powder, baking soda, and sugar until it is the texture of coarse meal. Add the buttermilk and continue to mix until a soft dough forms. Turn the dough out onto a clean, dry work surface and knead 4 to 6 times. The dough should be stiff but not sticky; add a little flour if necessary. Roll the dough out to 1 1/2 inches thick. Using either a 2 1/2-inch biscuit cutter or an empty baking powder can, which is the traditional cowboy tool, cut out the biscuits, re-rolling and cutting the remaining scraps, and place them on the prepared baking sheet a couple of inches apart. Let the biscuits rise at room temperature for 15 to 30 minutes, until doubled in size. Bake for about 15 minutes, until golden brown. Serve hot with butter or gravy.

VARIATION

For Buttermilk Pecan Biscuits, add 1 1/2 cups chopped pecans to the dry ingredients.

Hot Slaw

SERVES 4 TO 6

This is sort of like sauerkraut only it isn't sour; it's a little bit sweet. It's great on a burger or a steak sandwich.

2 tablespoons vegetable oil

$1/2$ red onion, minced

1 cup chopped bacon

$1/2$ head each red and green cabbage, shredded

$1/2$ cup cider vinegar

$1/4$ cup brown sugar

Salt

Freshly ground black pepper

Heat the oil in a large skillet over high heat until hot. Add the onion and bacon and sauté until the onion is soft and the bacon is crisp. Add the cabbage, vinegar, and sugar, and simmer over low heat for 15 to 20 minutes, until cabbage has softened. Season to taste with salt and pepper and serve hot—like the title says.

Grilled Corn with Spicy Lime Butter

SERVES 6

Grilled corn rubbed with a fresh lime is one of my favorite things to eat at Mexican street markets. Make this variation of an old Mexican tradition at your next barbecue.

6 ears fresh corn, left in the husks but silk
    tassels removed
$1/2$ cup butter
2 tablespoons freshly squeezed lime juice
1 tablespoon kosher salt
2 tablespoons chile powder

Place the corn in a large bowl, add enough cold water to cover, and let soak for 10 minutes. Prepare the grill according to the directions on page 15. Drain the corn in a colander, then grill for 10 to 12 minutes, turning occasionally, until the kernels are soft. Shuck the corn and set aside. In a small saucepan over medium heat, melt the butter. Add the lime juice, salt, and chile powder, and stir well. Remove from the heat and set aside. Return the shucked ears of corn to the grill for 5 minutes longer or until the kernels begin to blacken. Transfer the corn to a casserole dish and pour the lime-butter mixture over to cover. Serve hot.

Grilled Corn with
Spicy Lime Butter

Creamed Spinach

SERVES 4

I am convinced that creamed spinach was created just to go with beef. It is the perfect side dish for any kind of steak or roast. Always be sure to wash your spinach thoroughly, rinsing it several times to get rid of every trace of sand or grit.

4 tablespoons butter
1 pound fresh spinach, washed, trimmed,
    and torn into pieces
1/2 cup heavy whipping cream
2 tablespoons minced onion
1 clove garlic, minced
1 tablespoon flour
1 teaspoon sugar
Dash of grated nutmeg
1 teaspoon lemon juice
Salt
Freshly ground black pepper

In a large, heavy skillet over high heat, melt 2 tablespoons of the butter. Add the spinach, cover with a lid, and cook until it begins to steam, just a minute or so. Lower the heat and simmer 4 to 5 minutes longer, until the spinach is tender. Drain the spinach in a colander, then transfer to a food processor or blender and purée, being careful not to liquefy it. Set aside. Meanwhile, heat the cream in a small saucepan over medium heat until hot. Set aside. Melt the remaining 2 tablespoons of butter in the skillet set over high heat. Add the onion and garlic and sauté until soft. Slowly whisk in the flour until blended, then slowly add the hot cream and the sugar, whisking until smooth. Add the spinach and stir to combine. Add the nutmeg and lemon juice, and season to taste with salt and pepper. Serve hot.

RESOURCES

Branded Beef

B3R County Meats
P.O. Box 374
2100 West Highway 287
Childress, TX 79201
940-937-3668

California Beef Council
5726 Sonoma Drive, Suite A
Pleasonton, CA 94566-7751
925-484-2333
www.calbeef.org

Certified Angus Beef
206 Riffel Road
Wooster, OH 44691
330-345-2333

Certified Hereford Beef
P.O. Box 456
Red Oak, IA 51566
800-622-3083

Nolan Ryan's Tender Aged Beef
P.O. Box 448
Hunstville, TX 77342-0448
877-99-NOLAN

Sterling Silver
Excel Corporation
151 North Main
Wichita, KS 67202
800-621-0007

Texas Beef Council
8708 Ranch Road 620 North
Austin, TX 78726
www.txbeef.org

Mail Order

Allen Brothers
3737 South Halsted Street
Chicago, IL 60609-9882
800-957-0111

Balducci's
95 Sherwood Avenue
Farmingdale, NY 11735
800-225-3822

Omaha Steaks
4400 South 96 Street, P.O. Box 3300
Omaha, NE 68103
800-228-9055

Williams-Sonoma
P.O. Box 7456
San Francisco, CA 94120
800-541-2233

INDEX

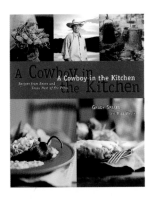
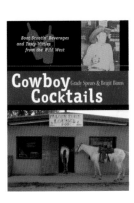